# A YEAR IN THE LIFE OF AN ABLE SEAMAN

Onboard HMS Warrior R31 (Air Craft Carrier) - 1954

Leslie Edward Smith

Copyright © 2022 Dawn Fallon

All rights reserved

No part of this book may be reproduced, or stored in a retrieval system, or transmitted in any form or by any means, electronic, mechanical, photocopying, recording, or otherwise, without express written permission of the publisher.

*Dedicated to my father - Leslie Edward Smith - and to the Carrickfergus Sea Cadets who are named after HMS Warrior which was built in Belfast.*

*Remembering all Personnel in the Armed Forces who have died during active service in conflicts and also during peacetime.*

*FOREVER IS COMPOSED OF NOWS*

                                    EMILY DICKINSON

# CONTENTS

| | |
|---|---|
| Title Page | |
| Copyright | |
| Dedication | |
| Epigraph | |
| Foreword | |
| Before Sailing - A Few Days Leave | 1 |
| Plymouth to Portsmouth & Bay of Biscay | 11 |
| Gibraltar to Malta | 17 |
| Malta to Port Said | 50 |
| Port Said to Aden | 57 |
| Aden to Ceylon (Sri Lanka) | 60 |
| Sri Lanka to Singapore | 67 |
| Singapore to Hong Kong | 79 |
| Hong Kong to Japan | 84 |
| Japan back to Singapore | 117 |
| Singapore to Haiphong | 130 |
| Haiphong to Hong Kong | 144 |
| Hong Kong to Singapore | 149 |
| Singapore to South Africa | 158 |
| South Africa to UK | 185 |
| Afterword | 191 |

# Acknowledgement

# FOREWORD

In 1954, my father (Leslie Edward Smith, Able Seaman, Gunnery - Navy Number D/SSX 860427), was given a 'Desk Diary' by Commander J. G. Wells for doing some special task. Les began writing in the diary when he was onboard HMS Warrior (R31). It says on the front cover 'With Compliments from K.B. Lee, Henry House, Hong Kong.' (The colour of the diary is red).

He records fairly mundane life onboard a ship - including his drunken escapades - but he also writes about the British Far East Fleet Exercise 'Operation Passage to Freedom' and the evacuation of Vietnam refugees in September 1954 and from that angle the diary may be of interest as a piece of naval history. The diary also records two casualties resulting in the loss of life of two pilots, demonstrating how dangerous some of the flying exercises were.

My father was born on 8 March 1931 in Bordesley Green, Birmingham and so he would have been 22-23 years of age when he kept this diary. He begins writing in it on Sunday 7 February 1954 and he wrote in it almost every day until 13 December 1954 - after which the entries stop.

My father joined the Royal Navy in 1949 (after being rejected the first time because he was too thin and underweight). He was from a very poor background and was one of the youngest of thirteen children. He often told me that he joined the navy in order to "get a decent pair of shoes", plus he wanted to see the world.

Overall he enjoyed navy life and found it an education to visit far away places with different cultures. Japan was his favourite country. He served for eight years in the Royal Navy as a gunner. Even though he candidly records his boredom onboard ship and some of the tedious jobs he was allotted - along with his frustration at being disciplined for several small misdemeanours - my father missed navy life when he was "de-mobbed" and he never did completely settle back fully into "civvy street" when he left in 1956. I think he missed the camaraderie he enjoyed on the ships, as well as the excitement of visiting new and foreign lands.

It became clear to me as I typed up the diary that the job he enjoyed most onboard was taking the ship's wheel for very short spells. I was surprised to read he did this job because as far as I know he was never trained in navigation.

I do not know what inspired my father to write in this diary.

After he left the navy I never knew him to write anything much at all, though it is clear from the diary that he often wrote letters to his family and to his fiancèe (my mother, Barbara) whilst he was in Service. So what the motivation for faithfully recording the minutiae of navy life as an Able Seaman for nearly a year is unclear. Perhaps it helped to ease his boredom - I never realised until reading his diary that boredom could be quite a problem for the lower ratings onboard ship.

Typing up the diary was quite emotional for me in many ways which I wasn't expecting, and it was a very interesting exercise. It felt quite intimate to type word by word the daily journey my father maps out of his navy life onboard this interesting ship. It was like meeting my 22-23 year-old father, and I felt I got to know him better. I typed up the diary when I was 60 years of age during the Covid lockdown in 2020, and my son (at the time of typing up the diary) was two years older than my father was when he penned his daily entries.

In the diary I learn that my father began his work on HMS Warrior as some kind of secretary typing up gunnery records. I never knew he could type. In fact he probably couldn't type properly as I doubt he was ever taught how to type at school, and I would imagine he typed using just two fingers, but it is obvious from the diary he did quite a lot of typing at one point. Why he was chosen for such a task I will never know. My father died in August 2010 and how I wish I had read the diary many years ago so that I could ask the many questions I now have.

The diary records detailed facts, but very few deep emotions - apart from feeling "chocker" (a naval term meaning "fed-up"). My father left school aged 14, so he didn't have the best of education, but he was not unintelligent. His handwriting, although not always legible, is elegantly formed and his spelling generally good - apart from the word "went" which he consistently misspelt as "whent" (I have corrected them all in the typescript), along with other minor spelling and grammatical errors (which I have left in). He had a unique way of forming the letter "d" and the letter "a" as a circle with a line

IX

alongside which I found to be distinctive - as illustrated below in the word "today" -

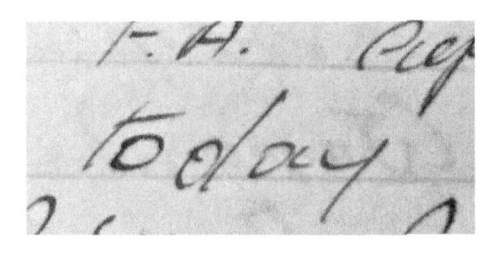

He was also fond of using ecphonesis, such as "Am I fed up!" or "How I hate the job!" or "And do I need it?!" - these are not questions, but rather an exclamation of his feelings, and his diary is peppered with these phrases. I rather enjoyed these unsolicited disclosures of emotion as my father, like many of his generation damaged by the trauma of war as a child, rarely expressed his feelings on a deep level.

My father uses a wide variety of naval slang and phrases which I have found to be fascinating, and these explained throughout the book as footnotes after each entry. I decided not to do a Glossary, but instead record the explanations of any unusual terms and words (which are in bold print) as the diary unfolds - and I hope this will spare any interested reader the inconvenience of having to constantly refer to a Glossary. I have also explained who some of the people are when my father mentions names of relatives, plus any facts and observations I thought might be useful as background information.

At times I felt quite envious that my father and his generation enjoyed something of a golden age in many ways in the 1950s. As an Epigraph for the diary I have chosen "Forever is composed of nows" by Emily Dickinson because this expresses something of what I felt coming through the pages as my father recorded all his "nows" with me picking them up over 65 years later and becoming totally absorbed in his world, the 50s era, and life onboard ship.

The actual diary has been passed down to my father's eldest

grandson - Ben - who kindly loaned it to me so that I could type it up. HMS Warrior (R31) has an interesting history and a good summary about this interesting ship can be read on Wikipedia online: https://en.wikipedia.org/wiki/HMS_Warrior_(R31).

**NOTES**:

*1) The Hong Kong Chamber of Commerce has a complete set of reports online (www.chamber.org.hk). The first mention of Henry House is in the 1953 report and it appears to be a building full of importers/exporters of china, textiles and other goods, even feathers, and their agents. Henry House was near Victoria Harbour, Hong Kong. The Henry House in the reports was on Ice House Street, but there's another on Yun Ping Road. There's no mention of K. B. Lee in the reports.*

*2) Videos - there are some videos of HMS Warrior on YouTube when she was owned by the Canadians but doing the same kind of stuff that my father describes: deck hockey, flying trials and refuelling. Crikey - not much room for the planes to land! The titles of the two videos on YouTube are: HMCS Warrior (R31) - Colossus Class Light Aircraft Carrier and 1940s Royal Canadian Navy Aircraft Carrier HMCS Warrior Visits Jamaica.*

**NOTE:** *If anyone can decipher the illegible words shown in the images where appropriate, or has any additional information or explanations of naval terminology, please get in touch with me (you can message my Facebook Page - Dawn Fallon, Author & Pianist)*

# BEFORE SAILING - A FEW DAYS LEAVE

***I must go down to the seas again, to the lonely sea and the sky.....***

From Sea-Fever, by John Masefield

(one of my father's favourite lines)

◆ ◆ ◆

*Sunday 7th February 1954*

Put my uniform on today, the first time for 3 weeks.

Went down to the "Drum" with Ron at 12 o'clock, met Jack and Frank in there, stayed till 2.

Went back to Ann's with Ron, found Barbara had left her engagement ring in Ann's because I was late in turning up (went to Jack's for dinner).

Went to "Golden Hind" on the night with Jack & Tom, met Ann & Ron in there (am I fed up!).

Saw Barbara at ten o'clock in Ann's, made it up with her and am feeling much better. I hope this never happens again.

**Notes:** *Ron was my father's brother-in-law - he was married to* my father's sister, Ann. Jack and Tom were my father's brothers. Barbara was my father's fiancée (also my mother - they married in 1955). I'm not sure who Frank was - possibly my father's older brother. The "Drum" and "Golden Hind" were pubs in Birmingham - they still exist to this day.

*Ann - my father's sister (and her husband Ron, my father's brother-in-law)*

DIARY OF AN ABLE SEAMAN - 1954

*My father with his brother, Tom, Malta 1949*

LESLIE EDWARD SMITH

*Jack - my father's brother (on his wedding day).*

DIARY OF AN ABLE SEAMAN - 1954

*Barbara & Les - Courting Days c.1954*

## Monday 8th February 1954

Returned today off my leave after 25 glorious days.

I caught the 1.30 train from New St. Tom and Jack came to the station with me, Tom was going to look for a job afterwards.

Borrowed a pound off Tom on the station, will send it to him pay day.

Left Ann's at 9.30 this morning after staying over night, reached home at 10.30 (was **chocker)**.

**Notes:** *As mentioned before, Tom and Jack were my father's brothers. Ann was his elder sister. "Chocker" is short for "Chock-A-Block" meaning "fed up".*

## Tuesday 9th February 1954

Reported to Sick Bay this morning to see if I was fit after being sick-on-shore. **M.O.** found nothing wrong?

Went to the pay office and drew my monthly issue of tobacco coupons, also checked my sick-on-shore pay and found I had £4 to come.

Had to go into Royal Naval Barracks at 10 o'clock for my tropical kit which consisted of:-
2 pair of white shorts
2 white fronts
1 pair of white shoes
1 pair of sandals
2 pair of blue shorts

Wrote to Barbara this evening have been thinking of her all day.

*Note:* M.O. = Medical Officer

## Wednesday 10th February 1954

Started to take onboard more ammunition today (bombs and rockets). Have enough ammo onboard here to win a war?

Received a letter from my beloved today, and she didn't seem very pleased with herself.

Went ashore at 7.30 - only had 7/6d so I went to the **Trelawney** in St Budeaux, had 3 pints of ale, then to a dance which I didn't enjoy one bit. Left dance at ten and went to the "Hot Dog" stall - had 2 Dogs and a cup of Oxo, then went aboard.

*Note:* *The Trelawney my father refers to was a pub (Trelawney Arms) in St Budeaux in Plymouth which closed in 2009 having a bad reputation, though what it was like in 1954 is not clear.*

## Thursday 11th February 1954

Still ammunitioning ship. I don't think our magazines will ever be filled.

Have been pretty busy today plenty of typing and so on.

Cleared lower deck at 1120 for payment - I drew £8.

Put my request in for a short weekend, I am hoping to catch the 1029 train on Saturday.

Stayed onboard this evening and had a quiet night (roll on Saturday).

## Friday 12th February 1954

Been very busy today amending ceremonial guide.

Was working until 8 o'clock for the Commander's office.

Got permission to proceed ashore at 0830 from the O.O.W (LT HAYWOOD).

I had a good run ashore tonight - first I went to the "BRITTANIA" *(sic.)* where I stayed till 9.45 then I went to the Embassy and had a very good time.

I lost my way walking back to the ship - I clued up in St. Budeaux instead of Devonport.

Arrived back onboard at 1 this morning feeling very tired.

**Note:** *O.O.W. - Officer of the Watch*

## Saturday 13th February 1954

Got permission to catch the 1028 train today. Left ship at 0945, got to North Road in time, caught train and arrived in Bristol at 2 o'clock, where I changed and caught the 2.12pm for Birmingham arriving here at 4.45pm. Went down home to find Mom, George, Fred and Tom in, gave Tom the £ I owed him, was pleased to hear Tom and Jack had got a job together?

Had my tea at home, then went to Barbara's, and was she surprised to see me, took her out for a drink with the gang in the "Hind" and had a smashing time. Went into Barbara's about

10.30pm and stayed till 1 o'clock.  Ann came round for me. Stayed at Mom's.

*Rosina - my father's mother (my grandmother)*

**Note:** *Fred, Tom & Jack were all my father's brothers.  Ann was his sister. George was likely my father's brother-in-law (George Lovell) who was married to my father's sister, Rose.*

### Sunday 14th February 1954

Got up at 9.30.  Ron made a pot of tea, had breakfast at 10.30, then started to get ready to go for a drink with Ron.

Went to the "Hind" where we met Jack and Frank, had a good drink.

Went back to Ann's and had dinner.  Barbara came round at 4, stayed in and watched T.V.  Ann gave Barbara and I some tea and put me up some food for going back.

LESLIE EDWARD SMITH

Ron and Ann didn't come for drink because Ron wasn't feeling so good (I think he drank too much at dinner time).

Had a nice drink with Barb, Rose, George and Tom. Caught the 1238 train back, felt grim. A foggy night in "Brum".

*Note: "Brum" is short for "Birmingham". Ann - my father's sister - obviously had a TV - quite unusual to own a TV in 1954, she and her husband Ron were publicans, so were often more well off compared to her siblings, she was a shrewd business woman and all the pubs she ran were very successful.*

# PLYMOUTH TO PORTSMOUTH & BAY OF BISCAY

*We sailed along together in the Bay of Biscay, Oh,
Where a dreadful storm it did arise and
the stormy wind did blow. I must go down to the
seas again, to the lonely sea and the sky.....*

(Traditional Sea Shanty - Bay of Biscay, O!)

*Warrior in Bay of Biscay (Rolling)*

❖ ❖ ❖

## Monday 15th February 1954

Arrived onboard at 7.35 this morning feeling very tired: got lined up and seen the O.O.W. usual procedure, Commander's report.

Left Plymouth at 3.20 for Portsmouth. I have got the Middle watch tonight.

Done my **dhobeing** and had a shower.

Wrote a letter to Barbara hoping it will get posted when we arrive at Portsmouth in the morning.

What a monotonous day this has been "Roll on 1956".

**Notes:** *Dhobeying (which my father often misspells) is a naval term meaning laundry.*

*1956 - this was the year my father was due to leave the navy. Although he refers to this fact, this entry highlights the fact that boredom was an issue for the lower ranks at times.*

## Tuesday 16th February 1954

Arrived in Portsmouth today at 6.30. Took passengers and **"AVGAS"** onboard - got underway at approx 1230.

**Make and mend** for me Middle watchman, slung my hammock at 1245 and turned in - had a smashing afternoon sleep - didn't get up until 4.30.

At 4.45 it was piped that the ship would be returning to Portsmouth as visibility is so bad that our Squadrons cannot fly on.

(No shore leave is being given). Wrote to Mom tonight as mail is being flown ashore by helicopter in the morning.

We are expecting to get under way about 6.30 in the morning.

*Notes: AVGAS - Aviation Gas*

*Make and Mend - naval term for half day off. It is derived from the time when sailors on sailing ships would often be allowed time to "make and mend" their uniforms.*

## Wednesday 17th February 1954

Got under way at 6.30 this morning. Squadron started to fly from Portsmouth.

The sea is rather choppy today.

Have been working on Ceremonial Orders all day, didn't finish work until 9 o'clock tonight.

## Thursday 18th February 1954

The sea is rather rough today, the ship has a steady roll on.

Done some flying trials this morning, one aircraft crashed into gun **sponson**, no casualties, but aircraft and one of the **Bofors** are in hell of a state.

Have completed the Ceremonial Orders today. Didn't finish work till 6 o'clock.

Have got the **first watch** tonight.

Ship is expected tor each the Bay of Biscay during the night, we are expecting some roughers so are battening everything down.

*Notes: Sponson - a platform built out from side of a ship - possibly a mounting point for aircraft.*

*Bofors - artillary*

*First Watch - it appears the ship operated a traditional watch system - these watches are divided into work periods by two teams over three days covering 24 hours, comprising: First Watch (2000-0000), Middle Watch (0000-0400), Morning Watch (0400-0800), Forenoon Watch (0800-1200), Afternoon Watch (1200-1600), First Dog Watch (1600-1800) and finally Second Dog Watch (1800-0000) to ensure that the roles are always occupied at all times.*

*A crashed Sea Fury FB11 on the flight deck of HMS Warrior*

## Friday 19th February 1954

Weather very rough this morning, scuttle in **For'cl Heads** caused in altered course in order to repair it.

Been busy on magazine log all day, will soon have it up to date.

Have got the middle watch tonight. I was late in mustering for sea boats crew, so had to do one hour lookout as punishment.

*Note: For'cl Heads - extreme forepart of forecastle structure.*

## Saturday 20th February 1954

The weather is much better today and we are running into a sunny climate.

Closed up for drill on the saluting guns at 1020 - fired a **7 gun salute** (for exercise).

Turned in this afternoon - was very tired after middle watch. Got up at 4.30 and turn to for 1 hour typing Gun Range Orders.

Clocks are being forwarded 1 hour tonight.

Ship is expected to arrive in Gibraltar at 0900 tomorrow morning.

Have got the morning watch.

*Note: 7 gun salute - normally it is a 21 Gun Salute, which is seven guns fired three times, but obviously they just fired 7 "for exercise" as there doesn't seem to be a 7 Gun Salute as such.*

LESLIE EDWARD SMITH

# GIBRALTAR TO MALTA

*The storm it being abated, we rigged up jury mast
And steered it for Gibraltar, where we arrived at last...*

(Traditional Sea Shanty - Bay of Biscay, O!)

◆ ◆ ◆

### Sunday 21st February 1954

Up at 4 this morning, was on the Q.D. preparing booms for lowering.

Secured at 6. Fell in on the flight deck for entering Gibraltar at 0830. Ship anchored at approx 0900. Postman was landed to bring off mail.

Received letter form Barbara, very pleased.

Ship got under way at 1.15 for Malta, weather wonderful. (Shore leave was not given to anyone at Gibraltar). Had a shower and done my dhobeing.

The ship's company changed in white caps today.

### Monday 22 February 1954

We are now in the sunny Med and the weather is first class.

Closed up for gun drill at 1030. Started flying at 1030, completed flying for the day at 1.45.

Have been working on the Magazine Log all day, turned to at 4 o'clock to do some typing for the Gunnery Officer.

Cleared out all my old mail.

The ship passed Algiers at 5.30 this evening, it was 15 miles to starboard.

Have got the first watch tonight, I hope I don't get caned for lookout.

*Defending HMS Warrior*

DIARY OF AN ABLE SEAMAN - 1954

*(Range Finder)*

### Tuesday 23 February 1954

Have been making up Magazine Max Temperature all day.

The weather has been just wonderful all day.

Had a shower and done my dhobeing, then I wrote a letter to Barbara, wish I was with her right now.

Have got the middle watch tonight. The ship is expected to arrive in Malta tomorrow morning.

### Wednesday 24th February 1954

Entered **Grand Harbour** at ten o'clock this morning, it was raining.

Had a make and mend this afternoon (middle watch) got my head down.

Received letter from Mom & Billy.

Went ashore at 5.30 with Evans from London. Went to Floriana and got very drunk, had a very nice evening. I spent 32/- spent most of the night in the "British Empire".

Had supper in Floriana. Slept ashore.

*Note: The Grand Harbour is a natural harour on the island of Malta. Floriana is a fortified town in Malta just outside the captial city of Valleta.*

*Billy was my father's younger brother.*

*Billy - circa 1960 (with his son, my cousin David)*

## Thursday 25th February 1954

Felt grim when I got up this morning, had a hangover. Caught the 7 o'clock boat back to the ship.

Didn't do much work today. I didn't feel up to the mark!!!

I soon got rid of my hangover when my **"TOT"** came up. Phoned up Ray Whale this evening. I am meeting him in **Sliema** tomorrow outside **Tony's Bar.** It will certainly bring back memories to me, because it is the place where Tom and I used to meet.

**Note:** "TOT" - This is the rum ration and was a daily amount of rum given to sailors on Royal Navy ships. It was abolished in 1970.

Sliema is a major residential and commercial area in Malta and a centre for shopping, bars and dining. Tony's Bar is situated on The Strand in Sliema - it is still there to this day.

Ray Whale was a friend of my father's. (I do not know how my father came to know Ray Whale who was in the Army and stationed at the Barracks in Malta - but it seems to have been through my father's younger brother Billy according to his next diary entry for 26th February).

## *Friday 26th February 1954*

Pay day today, picked up £4-10-0. Went ashore with Evans and Brum, had a few drinks in Floriana, then we went to Sliema and met Ray Whale (Billy's mate), had a few drinks in Sliema "Carolina Bar" then we all went back to Floriana and got proper drunk in the "British Empire". Finished up in the "Palladium" where we met two officers from the "Warrior" - had a couple of drinks with them then we went for Big Eats (Steak Eggs and Chips) 3/-

Left Ray in Floriana at 1 o'clock, slept ashore in the Golden Fleet lodging house.

## *Saturday 27th February 1954*

Got ordered at 0700 this morning had a horrible headache, couldn't eat my breakfast so just had a cup of tea. Thank God its Saturday and we have the afternoon off.

Done a small portion of typing this morning. Had my "TOT" and dinner, feeling much better. Turned in this afternoon till 5, then worked for another hour after which I went ashore and met Ray at his Barracks.

Went ashore in Sliema had some Beer and Eats. Caught a taxi

back at 12 o'clock, arrived onboard 1245.

Had a nice time ashore have got to see Ray tomorrow.

### Sunday 28th February 1954

Up at 7 this morning. Ship has got **C. in C's** inspection at divisions. My suit was to shoky* so I went to church in Floriana.

Came back from church at 12 had my dinner and "Tot" then went ashore and met Ray who came onboard for the afternoon. Had tea and supper onboard, then went ashore to Valletto to see the Carnival, got drunk down Kingsway.

Left Ray at 1245 - he went back to camp. I went down Floriana for some food, had steak and chips, met "Taff Pearce" and went back onboard with him.

*Note:* C.in C. - Commander in Chief. A commander-in-chief is the person who exercises supreme command and control over the ship (or any armed forces or military branch).
My father's reference to Church - he was brought up a Roman Catholic.

* Photo of illegible word 'shoky' ?

### Monday 1st March 1954

At sea today, left Grand Harbour at 0900 and proceeded for flying trials.

Felt very tired after my hectic run last night, haven't got a penny left!!! (never again).

Closed up this morning for Gun drill testing communications, etc.

Had a shower this evening and done my dhobeing, after which I wrote letter to Bill and Mom. Turned in at 0.30 feeling absolutely dead beat.

I think it only took me about five minutes before I was asleep. Ship dropped anchor in **MX** at approx 1830.

*Note:* MX - Marsamxett Harbour, just north of Grand Harbour, Malta

### Tuesday 2nd March 1954

**Weighed** and proceeded at 0700 this morning, continued with flying trials. Closed up for tracking of 4 sea fury aircraft for one hour.

Received letter from Barbara this evening, was very pleased to hear from her.

Captain made a speech to the ship's company regarding our pay, have found out that I am now 1/- per day better off "What a Navy".

Ship dropped anchor in MX at 1830 this evening.

There was a Dinner Show onboard tonight, shame I didn't go owing to financial difficulties.

Borrowed 2/6 off "Mick" Mills for laundry.

*Note: Weighed - weigh anchor is a nautifcal term meaning raising the anchor of the ship indicating the final preparation for getting underway.*

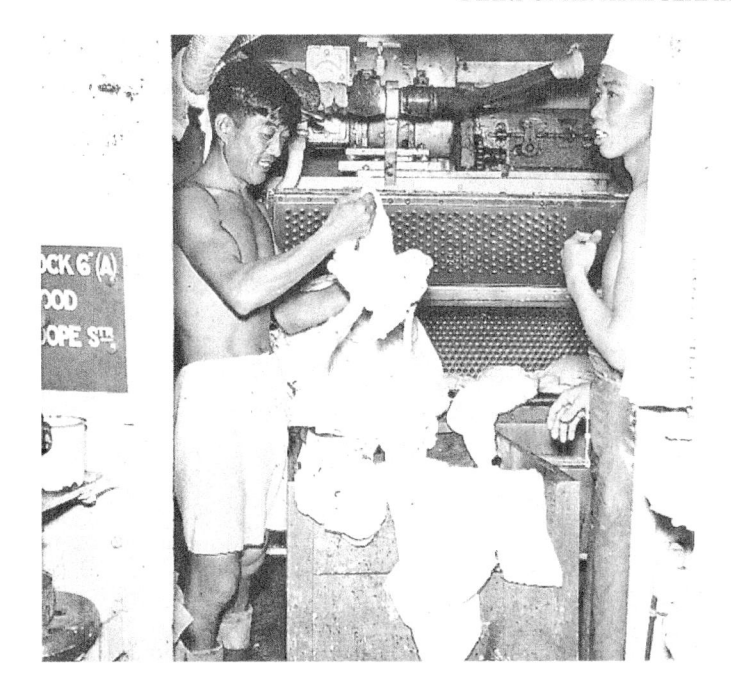

*HMS Warrior's Laundry*

## Wednesday 3rd March 1954

Weighed anchor at 0715 and proceeded for further flying trials.

Closed up for gun drill at 0945 for half hour.

Two aircraft crashed with minor damage.

The hands had a make and mend (I turned to)!!!

The ship was to return to MX at 1600 but the weather was too rough for us to get in so we remained at sea all night.

I have got the middle watch. During the middle watch at approx. 0030 we received distress signal from a Norwegian merchant ship so we proceeded to her aid, her bearing was North, 70 miles off Malta.

Received further signal at 0354 saying we were not required as she was safe.

*__Note:__ Closed-up - this refers to the ship being fully 'closed up' with weapons manned - possibly meaning all hatches, doors etc closed to ensure watertight integrity.*

*Gun Crew Closed Up - HMS Warrior (1953)*

## Thursday 4th March 1954

The sea today was still rough.

The ship was to anchor in MX at 1130 today but another ship had taken our berth, so "Warrior" remained at sea.

Closed up for briefing by the Gunnery Office at 0945 on the Q.D. we were lectured on Gyro Gun sights.

Had a make and mend today (middle watch) - turned in my hammock at 1300, got up again at 1700.

Went down the office at 1900 to type Gunnery programme for tomorrow - Friday - finished at 2000.

I have got the morning watch.

### Friday 5th March 1954

Up at 4 this morning, lookout on the bridge from 5-6 then I secured.

Ship entered MX we disembarked some of our aircraft, then we got underway again. Done a shoot on the Bofors.

Entered Grand Harbour at 1530, fired a 17 Gun salute for Lord Louis Mountbatten.

Have been "chocker" all day today. Have put in for a change of jobs.

(Roll on my time).

### Saturday 6th March 1954

Saturday routine today negative Captain's rounds. Entered Max. temp in part I of Magazine Log.

Captain cleared lower deck at 1140 gave speech to ship's company.

Listened to football match on wireless (B'ham v Bristol R.) match was drawn 1-1.

Pressed my suit this evening for divisions.

Roll on next week to get some money.

Received a letter from Barbara. I was not expecting one.

**Note:** *Negative Captain's Rounds or Negative Divisions means there would have been no Divisions (Parade) on this day.*

### Sunday 7th March 1954

Worked for 1 hour this morning then I went to divisions which were held on the flight deck.

C. in C. Med came onboard (Admiral Mountbatten) he gave a speech to the ship's company. Then we marched past.

Played dominoes today won 1/3d am now a **baron** !!!

Had a shower and done my dhobeying this evening.

The ship has been open to visitors all day.

*Note: Use of the word "baron" - my father was skint at the time, so the meagre winnings of 1/3d were therefore not to be sneered at because that sum would have lifted him from abject poverty to a degree of richness worthy of a 'baron'. The 'Baron' handle was applied to any messmate who was better off than oneself, even if only by the slim margin of a few coins.*

### Monday 8th March 1954

I am 23 years of age today. I had **sippers** from all the lads in the mess (felt rather drunk).

Received a birthday card and a letter from Barbara this evening.

The ship has been at sea all day today doing our usual flying trials.

Closed up for Gunnery exercise at 1600 done some tracking on A/C.

Anchored in MX at 1730.

Went to the pictures with "Mick" Mills. The film was "Blowing Wild" it was quite good.

*Note: A/C = Aircraft.*

*Sippers - A sip from a messmate's tot of rum and became a customary birthday gift to a lucky sailor from all his messmates.*

## Tuesday 9th March 1954

Got underway at 0730 this morning there were 1 WREN officer and 11 Wrens came onboard for the day.

One of our A/C pitched into the sea at 1330. It was piloted by the squadron leader. Both pilot and observer were picked up by helicopter, there were no casualties.

The ship anchored in MX at 1700, there was no shore leave given owing to rough weather.

One of our lads was landed onshore at 2330 this evening for Royal Naval hospital, he had pneumonia.

## Wednesday 10th March 1954

Ship was underway at 0730 with usual WRENS onboard.

A.B. Elan came down the office all day, he is taking over my job as gunnery office writer. I am going to be **M.A.A.'s** Messman.

Took an unofficial make and mend this afternoon got my head down till 1600.

We exercised darken ships tonight for the first time all went well.

The ship anchored in MX at approx 1700.

No mail today (chocker).

We fired break up shot at A/C this morning, all went to plan.

*Note: M.A.A. - Master-At-Arms, the chief of the ship's police. I remember my father telling me a story about the Master At Arms - I do not know if it was when he was on the Warrior or some other ship, but there was an Officer called Buglehole, and the Master-At-Arms used to call him "Trumpet Arse". This greatly amused my father who thought it was very funny. Also he was quite amused by one of the Chinese laundrymen who couldn't pronounce*

"Master At Arms" but would call him "Marratahm". My father loved words and any twist or mispronounciation of them gave him untold pleasure.

### Thursday 11 March 1954

I am no longer Gunnery Office Writer. Work over MAAs Messman at 0830 this morning. I have yet to get settled in.

Ship got underway at approx 0730, carried on with flying. One aircraft crashed in the sea at 1010, the pilot and observer were picked up by helicopter, the observer had broken arm.

Ship anchored at 1220 in MX. Flying for the day was abandoned.

Went to the cinema onboard with "Brum" to see "Call Me Madame" I enjoyed it very much.

### Friday 12th March 1954

Ship remained in MX until 1300 then we proceeded to Grand Harbour (Exercised **D.C. State 1**)

Entered Grand Harbour at 1500 with usual Guard and Band playing, secured at 1530.

Cleared lower deck for payment on securing. I got paid £4=10=00.

Feeling rather fed up tonight so I read through some of Barbara's old letters which helped to cheer me up a little.

Did not go onshore I have got to save my money!!!

*Note: D.C. State 1 - a term used onboard ship: Damage Control State 1 means Action Stations and implies ship could have been under attack (at war) or it was going through exercises to simulate as such.*

### Saturday 13 March 1954

I seem to be getting settled in quite nicely as MAA's Messman.

Had Captain's rounds today. Got **"Jaunty's"** and **RPOs** messes up to date for rounds, all went well.

Stayed onboard this evening and played Ludo with the boys.

What a life roll on my time.

*Notes: Jaunty - traditional nickname for the Master-At-Arms.
RPO - Regulating Petty Officer*

## Sunday 14th March 1954

Divisions today, Captain's inspection. I was excused.

Received three letters today, one from Barbara, one from Mom and one from Billy and was I pleased.

Went on the flight Deck this afternoon and did some sun bathing, the weather is absolutely great.

We heard today that the ship is going on a cruise during the Easter period to Venice.

I think I am going to enjoy that very much.

I have never been to Venice before, it is wonderful.

## Monday 15 March 1954

Left Grand Harbour at 0900 this morning, proceeded to sea for flying trials.

Had a briefing on Gun drill etc by the Gunnery Officer.

The ship anchored in MX at 1700. The weather today has been very nice.

Wrote a letter to Barbara also sent her a blouse.

I got a new Pay Book today. Whilst I was doing my routine I scalded my foot in the Sick Bay.

### Tuesday 16th March 1954

We got underway at 0800 this morning.

16 Wrens came onboard for the day. More flying trials. I am beginning to get chocker with this!!!! Anchored in MX at 1700.

The sea today has been rather rough (quite a heavy swell).

Went to the pictures this evening with Evans, the film being shown was "Roman Holiday".

One aircraft crashed into the Barrier - smashed his prop up.

*Note: "prop" I assume is propeller.*

### Wednesday 17th March 1954

We got underway at 0800 again today - more Wrens came onboard.

Closed up for 40 MM Bofors firings this morning. I did not fire owing to my gun being damaged.

The ship anchored in MX at 1700. I was going ashore but I changed my mind at the last minute. Roll on UK.

Wrote letters to Mom & Billy this evening.

The sea today has been much better than it was yesterday, in fact it was practically flat.

### Thursday 18th March 1954

Remained in MX all forenoon. Carried out General drill exercise. I had two "Tots" today, good oh.

The ship proceeded to Grand Harbour at 1515.

Had a shower and did some dhobeying. I had a quiet evening

onboard.

Had my hair cut today and it is exceptionally short. If Barbara could see me now I wonder what she would say?

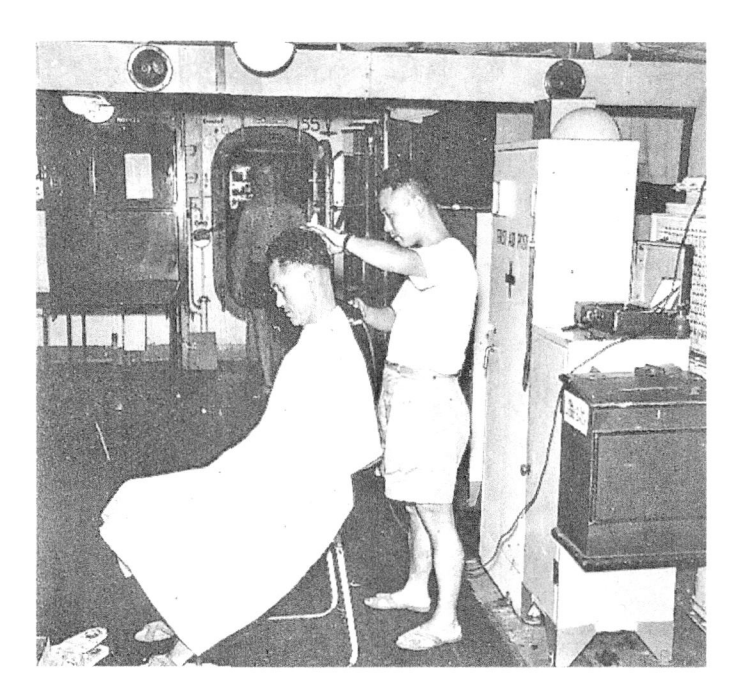

*HMS Warrior Barber*

## Friday 19th March 1954

Scrubbed paintwork in the RPO's mess this forenoon, getting on top line for rounds tomorrow.

Lent "Brum" Seager £1 and went ashore with him to Floriana. Had quite a crop of beer tonight got rather drunk. Brum and I went for Big Eats.

I phoned Ray up when I got ashore, but he never turned up. I can't make out what could have happened to him.

Slept ashore - we were a little too drunk to go back onboard ship!!!

## Saturday 20th March 1954

Up at 6.30 this morning feeling on top of the world?

Caught the 0700 Boat back.

Started to get the R.P.O's & MAA's messes ready for rounds, everything went well.

Got my head down this afternoon, had a smashing sleep. I didn't get up till 5.30.

All the R.P.O's are ashore tonight so I have nothing to do, just the job.

Had my supper from the Wardroom Galley (Big Eats).

## Sunday 21st March 1954

Had my photo taken for my service certificate, also saw my service papers - usual report **(V.G. Sat)**. It has been a lovely day today, I have been on the flight deck all afternoon.

All the R.P.Os are ashore again today, nothing to do?

Had a shower at 4 o'clock and did some dhobeing.

Played **(Uckers)** Ludo with the lads in the mess this evening.

**Notes:** "V.G.Sat." = Very Good / Satisfactory. Seems to have been the normal report for most seamen.

"Uckers" is a board game for two to four players traditionally played in the Royal Navy and is similar to the game of Ludo (as my father notes).

DIARY OF AN ABLE SEAMAN - 1954

*One of my father's reports*

## Monday 22 March 1954

Slipped from our buoys in Grand Harbour at 0900 and proceeded to sea for flying trials.

When we got to sea we found out there was not enough wind to do flying, so trials were scrubbed for the day.

The weather has been perfect today.

Ship anchored in MX at 1300. The hands went to bathe over the side at 1600.

Went to the pictures this evening, the film:- "War of the Worlds" quite a good show.

## Tuesday 23rd March 1954

The ship got underway at approx 0730 assuming D.C. State (1).

Flying trials were continued, everything going smoothly. The wind today was fairly strong but ideal for flying.

Gun crews closed up for firing at a **sleeve target,** the shot went off very well. One sleeve was shot down during the first run a second sleeve was shot down some 15 minutes later (Big recommends for the Gun Crews).

The ship anchored in MX at 1700.

The hands were **piped** to bathe.

**Notes:** *Sleeve Target - a tubular cloth target towed by an airplane for use in air and ground anti-aircraft gunnery practice.*

*Piped - the Boatswain's call (or whistle) is a naval instrument used for ceremony and for sound signalling orders and commands throughout the ship.*

## Wednesday 24th March 1954

Put to sea again at 0730 flying trials being resumed. Aircraft were firing at splash target which was being lowered by ourselves.

Gun crews closed up again today for another shoot at a sleeve target, one sleeve being shot down.

The ship anchored at 1630 in MX.

Captain made a speech to ship's company informing us that we may be required to escort HM the Queen into Aden, round about April the 21st.

DIARY OF AN ABLE SEAMAN - 1954

*Splash Target practice onboard HMS Warrior 1954*

## Thursday 25th March 1954

Got underway at 0730, flying trials continued, aircraft resumed firings at splash target, all went well.

The ship is expected to remain at sea all night. I have the last day and all night in!!!

The ship's company were paid at 1800 on the Flight Deck. I drew £4=10=0.

I haven't received any mail for 12 days. I hope there is some mail for me tomorrow?

Cleaned my locker out today and it looks very neat. I hope I can keep it that way !!

## Friday 26th March 1954

The ship has been at sea all night.

Commenced flying trials at approx 0800.

One aircraft crashed through two barriers - aircraft completely smashed up, the pilot got out unhurt.

Received a letter from Barbara this afternoon (mail was brought onboard by helicopter).

The ship anchored in the MX at 1745, no leave was given as it was too rough for our boats to be lowered.

Had a shower this evening and washed my shifts.

*Note: My father always referred to his underwear as 'shifts'. I remember that he always used to have his 'clean shifts' ready after his weekly bath on a Friday night.*

## Saturday 27th March 1954

The ship remained anchored in MX today.

Normal Saturday routine - Captain's rounds.

The semi-final of the cup was played today, the scores were:-
WBA 2 - Port Vale 1
Sheff WD 0 - **P.N.E.** 2

The Grand National was also seen being won by the Irish horse Royal Tan.

The weather has been rough in MX all day. Anchor watches are being kept.

*Note: P.N.E. - Preston North End*

## Sunday 28th March 1954

Anchored in MX all day.

Normal Sunday routine, negative divisions.

Wrote a letter to Barbara.

It has been a very quiet day today - nothing special happening.

The evening mail came onboard at 1900 I had a letter from Mom.

Had a shower and did my dhobeying.

## Monday 29th March 1954

Put to sea at 0730, carried on with flying exercises. Aircraft machine Gun splash target.

Received a signal telling us to proceed to Grand Harbour, but the weather was too rough for us to get in so we anchored in MX.

There seems to be something happening somewhere as the ship is at 4 hours notice. We disembarked our wrecked aircraft.

D.C. State (1) was exercised today.

## Tuesday 30 March 1954

Got underway at 0700 did some flying until 1200 when we entered Grand Harbour where we started to embark "AVGAS" stores etc.

Leave was given until 2359 so I decided to have a run ashore.

Had a shower first then I caught the 1830 boat.
Went to Floriana where I stayed all night.

Came back onboard at 0130 making me one and half hours adrift. Usual procedure Commander's report.

The ship has been at 4 hours notice all day.

## Wednesday 31st March 1954

Have got a thick head this morning never again!!!

Saw the Commander, he gave me Captain's report. Saw the Captain at 1000 and he gave me 5 day leave stopped + 1 day pay - am I chocker.

The ship left Grand Harbour at 1500 for exercise off Tunisia, we are at sea all night I have the middle watch.

There seems to be a little trouble in Egypt but things seem to have quietened a little now.

*Note: "a little trouble in Egypt" refers to the 1954 government crisis under General Neguib - video footage can be seen on Pathe News - www.britishpathe.com/video/general-neguib-government-crisis*

## Thursday 1 April 1954

Had a horrible middle (watch).

Started to fly off at 0630 this morning.

One aircraft crashed into the sea half a mile from the Tunisian shore, the Pilot **(Sub. Lt. Evans)** was killed.

The ship anchored at 1500 near the scene of the crash and divers were sent down, the aircraft was in bits, it had evidently blown up, there was no sign of the pilot. We gave up hopes of the search and got underway at 2000.

Sub. Lt. Evans was only 21 years of age and had only joined our squadron 2 days ago.

*Note: This was Sub. Lt. Derek B. Evans in the loss of Sea Fury VW652. I never realised so many Servicemen died during peace time. 120 Royal Navy men died in 1954 (from accident, illness or training exercises).*

## Friday 2nd April 1954

Had the morning watch, was lookout from 0400 to 0500. Secured at 0600.

Started to fly off at 0630, carried out exercises till 1600 then we anchored in MX. Leave was given till 2359.

Had my head down all afternoon. I had rather a large "TOT" which made me feel tired.

Lent "Brum" Seager £1 - it will help me to save towards Barbara's watch.

## Saturday 3rd April 1954

Normal Saturday routine negative rounds.

Could not go ashore today am still under punishment!!

The Oxford and Cambridge boat race was run today being won by Oxford.

Also England beat Scotland in the international match at Hampden Park today, the score was 4-2.

England's goals were scored by:-
Broad, Nicolls, Allen, Mullen.

The attendance was 134,000.

## Sunday 4th April 1954

Normal Sunday routine negative divisions.

A memorial service was held onboard for Sub.Lt. Evans. Captain addressed the ship's company.

Had my photo taken today on the flight deck.

The Ship's side was prepared for painting. Ray Whale phoned me up this evening but I could not go ashore as I am still under punishment!!

Wrote a letter to Mom. The ship's company started to wear white fronts today.

## Monday 5th April 1954

The hands were employed in scrubbing the ship's side today.

Finished my punishment today and am I glad.

The weather has been grim all day, it has been very dull and it rained this evening.

The lads started an "Uckers" competition, the winner gets 16/-

Wrote a letter to Barbara this evening, I am rather late in answering her last letter.

Spent my last 2/6d on a tin of tobacco today, its a good job we get paid this Friday!!

*Painting the ship's side - HMS Warrior 1954*

### Tuesday 6th April 1954

Went ashore at 1830 with "Flossie" Ford. Went to Valleta and down the **"GUTT"** *(sic.)* there were not many blokes ashore.

Stayed down the "GUTT" all evening, got very drunk.

Had big eats in Ben-Marks, spaghetti and lobster, good-oh.

Stayed ashore all night in lodging house.

*Note:* *See photo below of "The Gut" which is in Strait Street, Valetta. It has quite a colourful history and in the 1950's was seen as rather seedy, sleazy but fun place to be and many sailors hung out there. The Gut is still going today but in a different manner. It has a Facebook Page.*

## Wednesday 7th April 1954

Felt pretty grim this morning, I was up at 6 o'clock.

Caught the 7 o'clock boat back to the ship.

Did not do much work this morning.

When I got back onboard I found there was a letter for me from my old mate Darby Allen. I was quite pleased to hear from him.

The ship's company had inoculations today for yellow fever and cholera. We have more to come yet. Answered Darby's letter this evening.

Had a shower and a bath and did some dhobeying.

## Thursday 8th April 1954

Was sent outside the Reg Office this morning for slack hammock but the RO let me off with it.

The hands have been painting ship again today.

The weather has been grim all day, it rained very hard this evening.

Sent my hammock, bed covers etc to the laundry.

Wrote a letter to Bill this evening and told him the date we are expecting to arrive in **Port Said**.

*Note:* Port Said is a city that lies in north east Egypt along the coast of the Mediterranean Sea north of the Suez Canal.

## Friday 9 April 1954

Pay day today, and do I need it? Had £3 paid back to me what was owing.

Got picked up for hair cut at the **pay table**.

Went ashore at 1530. Went to Floriana. I met Evans in the Coronation Bar where we had a few bottles. From there we went to the British Empire where we met L.P.M. Summer and L.P.M. Churchill.

I got really drunk in there, we then went to the Klondyke where we had a few more bottles, then we all went to the Palladium where I met Jess* who I knew in Plymouth and was I surprised, we caught a taxi and I took her home good oh!!!

**Note:** *There used to be 'Pay Parades' where each rating had to march up to the pay table in turn, salute, give name and service number, after which an enveloped with the rating's name on would be handed over. The rating would then salute again and march off. The last Royal Navy Pay Parade was on 16 January 1986 and from then on pay was paid into bank accounts. The Pay Parades were also used to inspect uniforms and physical appearance, hence my father got picked up for needing a hair cut at the pay table.*

*\*I have no idea who Jess was, my father never spoke of her. She may have been an old flame, but they certainly struck up a renewed friendship in Sliema! (Reading between the lines!)*

## Saturday 10th April 1954

Got back onboard at 0320 this morning and crashed under the table. I got up at 0620 and was I tired.

There was no Captain's round today thank God!!

Got ready and went ashore, met Jess at Sliema outside Tony's, took her to the pictures to see "Bitter Rice".

I went up to her mate's flat afterwards, had tea. Jess and I stayed in all evening, her mate went out. We had quite a pleasant evening together.

I stayed at the flat for a night as it was too late for me to get back onboard.

## Sunday 11th April 1954

I did not get up till 0700 this morning and my leave expired at 0715. I did not get onboard till 0805. I was took before the Officer of the Watch (Mr King), he gave me Commander's report, am I chocker.

The ship is open to visitors today. There was not any divisions.

I turned in right after dinner as I was dead tired.

Got up at 1745 feeling much better.

I wanted to go ashore this evening but the **"jaunty"** would not let me go being a reported leave breaking offence and I was supposed to have seen Jess this evening.

***Note:*** *"Jaunty" - Master-At-Arms (head of ship's police).*

## Monday 12th April 1954

Saw the Commander this morning and was he cut up, he gave me Captain's report whom I saw straight away, my punishment was 5 days leave stopped and one days pay forfeited.

Jess phoned me up at 1400 wanting to know why I did not go ashore yesterday.

She wanted me to go ashore this evening, but it is impossible.

I had a shower after supper and I did some dhobeying, feeling rather fed up not being able to go ashore.

## Tuesday 13th April 1954

Today has been rather dull. Nothing exceptional has been happening.

The routine today has been paint ship which is nearly completed - it is only a matter of the side being touched up here and there.

The weather today has been the same as my routine, dull, with the sea in the Grand Harbour "choppy".

Wrote a letter to Barbara this evening, it's about time too, I am five days late in answering her last letter.

It has been piped this evening that there will be no issue of mail.

## Wednesday 14th April 1954

The Fleet entered Grand Harbour today after their Spring Cruise. The "Gutt" should be pretty busy tonight.

It has been raining all day with quite a strong wind blowing, the **"Dqhaisas"** stopped running owing to rough weather.

The ship is now completely painted and we are all ready for our trip to the Far East.

I lent "Scouse" Whittle £1 so he could have a run ashore. I might as well, I can't go myself?

*Note*: Dqhaisas was possibly a shuttle boat or tender transporting the men to shore.

## Thursday 15th April 1954

The ship came back into routine today after 2 weeks self maintenance.

The weather has not changed much today, still raining and dull.

Received two letters today, one from Mom and one from Barbara.

Barbara gave me quite a dressing down for only writing her small letters and getting drunk!!

The way things are going I think she will be packing me in.

Roll on Hong Kong!

## Friday 16th April 1954

Sunday routine today (Good Friday), the hands secured at 0900 and leave was given.

Got my head down on the Gun **Sponson** this afternoon. At 1300 HMS Eagle entered Grand Harbour.

Had a shower and did my dhobeying. Tonight is the last night of my punishment.

There is a great improvement in the weather today, the sun was shining and it was quite warm.

***Note***:  *Sponsons are projections extending from the sides of aircraft or watercraft to provide protection, stability, storage locations, or equipment housing.*

# MALTA TO PORT SAID

*"The Navy had always regarded Malta as the keystone of victory in the Mediterranean, and considered it should be held at all costs."*

Admiral Andrew Browne Cunningham, Commander-in-Chief of the Mediterranean (1939)

◆ ◆ ◆

## Saturday 17th April 1954

Took onboard stores, fresh water, passengers etc this morning.

We slipped from No.5 berth Grand Harbour at 1045 for Port Said.

Our squadrons flew onboard at 1200, one aircraft crashed through the two barriers, no casualties.

The sea is choppy and there is a strong wind blowing.

Make and mend this afternoon so I got my head down seeing I have the morning watch.

Turned in my hammock early and read a **"Hank Janson"**.

*Note: Hank Janson books were violent pulp fiction thrillers with Hank being a tough Chicago reporter written by the English author Stephen Daniel Frances. Frances wrote over 300 of the books between 1946 and 1971. Many of the often lurid covers were created by Reginald Webb, who often signed his work as Reginald Heade.*

## Sunday 18th April 1954

Up at 0400 this morning, sea boats crew, the PO did not call my name so I did not get a lookout?

Secured at 0600. The sea today is fair and the wind has dropped, the ship has a steady roll on.

Got my head down this afternoon, nothing else to do. Got up at 1600.

Had a shower this evening and done some dhobeying.

Have got all night in tonight.

## Monday 19th April 1954

Commenced flying at 0900 this morning.

Closed up for Saluting Run drill this morning at 1030.

Received a "JAB" - cholera, its pretty painful too.

Secured from flying stations at 1300 for the day as the ship has too much of a roll on.

I have got the first watch tonight, am I "chocker".

The ship will be entering Port Said tomorrow forenoon.

## Tuesday 20th April 1954

The ship entered Port Said at 1045 this morning, we anchored just outside the harbour awaiting our turn to go through the Canal.

We did not stay in Port Said at all, we entered the Canal at approx 1530 going straight through.

I received a letter from Bill saying he had been waiting in Port Said all morning.

30 troops of the airborne division came onboard at P. Said for passage to Suez.

Closed up on the gun for the last dog. I also have the middle, the ship anchored in the Bitter Lakes at about 1130.

*Note:* *Bill was my father's brother and he was in the Army - they had obviously arranged to meet up in Port Said but in the end obviously the ship didn't stop there.*

## Wednesday 21 April 1954

We got underway at 0330 this morning, I went off watch at 0400.

Got up at 0630 feeling rather tired after the middle watch. The ship anchored in Port Suez at 0830 and we disembarked Army personnel. We met HMS Wakeful at Suez.

The ship got underway at 0930 and we entered the Red Sea. The sun was rather dull but very warm with quite a cool breeze blowing. Got my head down this afternoon.

I turned in at 1300 and slept until 1730 and did I need it.

The heat below decks this evening reached about 90 degrees.

I have the morning watch.

## Thursday 22 April 1954

Up at 0400 this morning, was lookout on the bridge from 0530 to 0600 after which I secured.

Closed up for saluting gun drill this morning ready for when we meet HM The Queen.

The weather today has been very hot with the temperature reaching 92 degrees below decks.

The ship should be nearing Abyssinia some time tomorrow.

Slung my hammock on the FX this evening, it is far too hot to sleep below decks.

## *Friday 23 April 1954*

Got up this morning feeling very clammy "What a climate".

Went to flying stations at 0800, we flew both squadrons off, handing on again at 1200.

Cleared lower deck at 1500 and exercised "Man and cheer ships" for when we meet the **"Gothic"**.

The hands were paid on the flight deck on completion of the exercise. I was paid £6=0=0d in Maltese currency.

The weather has been warmer today temperature below decks 96 degrees and in the Galley 160.

I have the first watch tonight, relieved the Q.M. on the wheel.

**Note:** *Q.M. - QuarterMaster.*

SS *Gothic was passenger-cargo liner and became famous when she was designated a royal yacht from 1952 to 1954.*

## *Saturday 24th April 1954*

Had the middle watch last night feeling very tired this morning.

We had a full dress rehearsal for **"Man & Cheers ship"** the hands cleaned into **No 6's** and were inspected by DOs, I was picked up for a hair cut.

We fired a 21 gun salute (for exercise).

Got my head down on the FX this afternoon, there was a smashing breeze blowing.

We have been passing a series of volcanic Islands all day.

The weather has been grim, temperature below decks 96 degrees.

*Note:* "Man & Cheers ship" - to salute a passing ship from sailors stationed on the deck (generally aircraft carriers were manned six feet from the edge of the flight deck) - usually holding their caps out in front.

No. 6's was reference to a type of uniform - there were No. 2's and No.10's also.

*1960s No 6 tropical jacket*

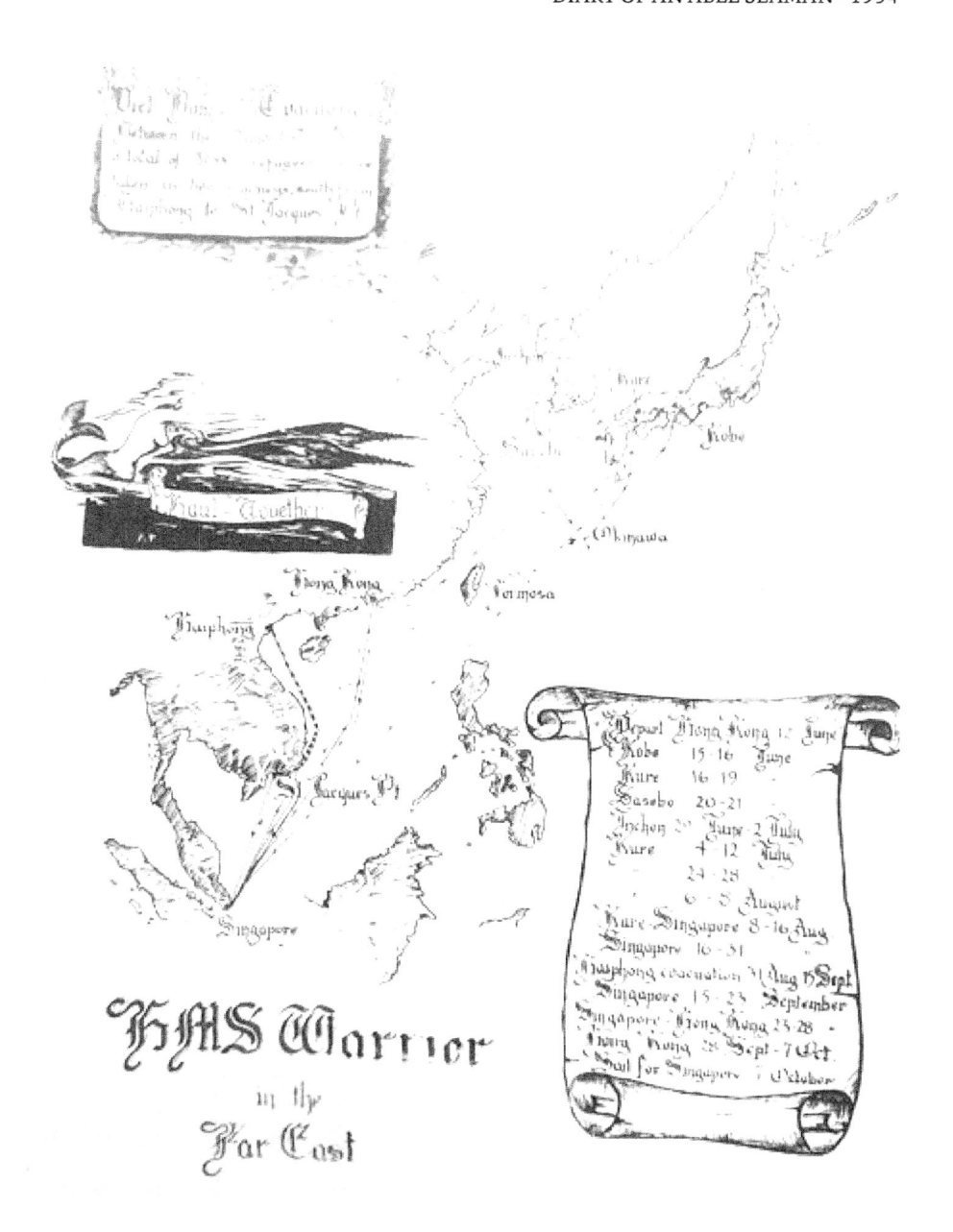

DIARY OF AN ABLE SEAMAN - 1954

HMS Warrior
in the
Far East

Depart Hong Kong 12 June
Kobe 15-16 June
Kure 16-19
Sasebo 20-21
Inchon 22 June-2 July
Kure 4-12 July
24-28
6-8 August
Kure-Singapore 8-16 Aug
Singapore 16-31
Haiphong evacuation 31 Aug-13 Sept
Singapore 15-23 September
Singapore-Hong Kong 23-28
Hong Kong 28 Sept-7 Oct
Sail for Singapore 7 October

LESLIE EDWARD SMITH

# PORT SAID TO ADEN

*(through the Suez Canal, down the Red Sea)*

### *Sea Calm*

*How still,*
*How strangely still*
*The water is today,*
*It is not good*
*For water*
*To be so still that way.*

Langston Hughes

◆ ◆ ◆

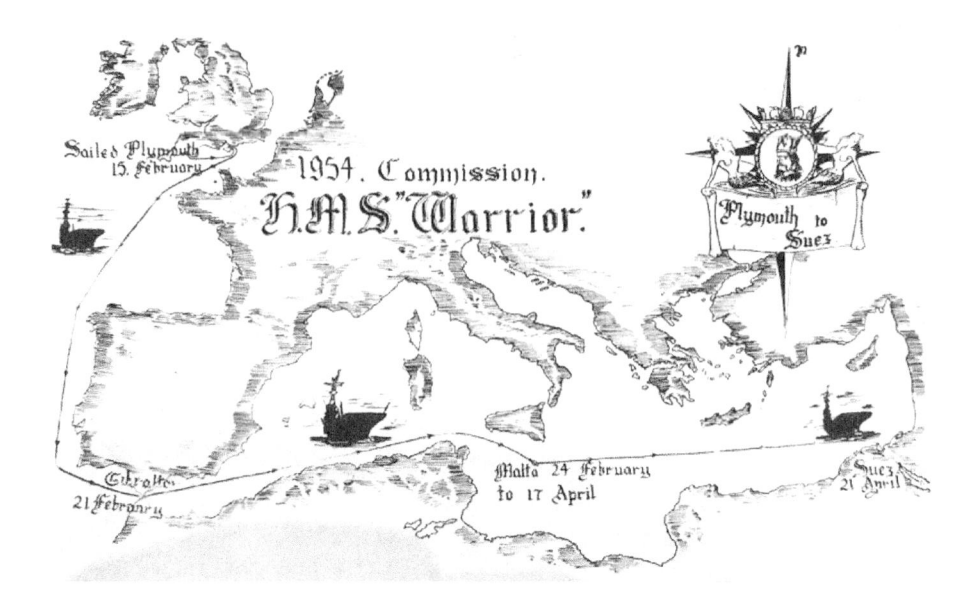

## Sunday 25th April 1954

The ship entered Aden at 0837 this morning, securing to 4 buoys.

Aden is completely trimmed up ready for the visit of HM the Queen.

Took on oil fuel, fresh water and 9 tons of veg.

The hands were scrubbing the starboard side because that is the side the Queen will see as we go past.

There was plenty of trading going on over the ships side today. I did not buy anything. We left Aden at 1645 for Ceylon.

I have the morning watch.

DIARY OF AN ABLE SEAMAN - 1954

# ADEN TO CEYLON (SRI LANKA)

*"Till noon we quietly sailed on,
Yet never a breeze did breathe:
Slowly and smoothly went the ship,
Moved onward from beneath."*

Samuel Coleridge Taylor

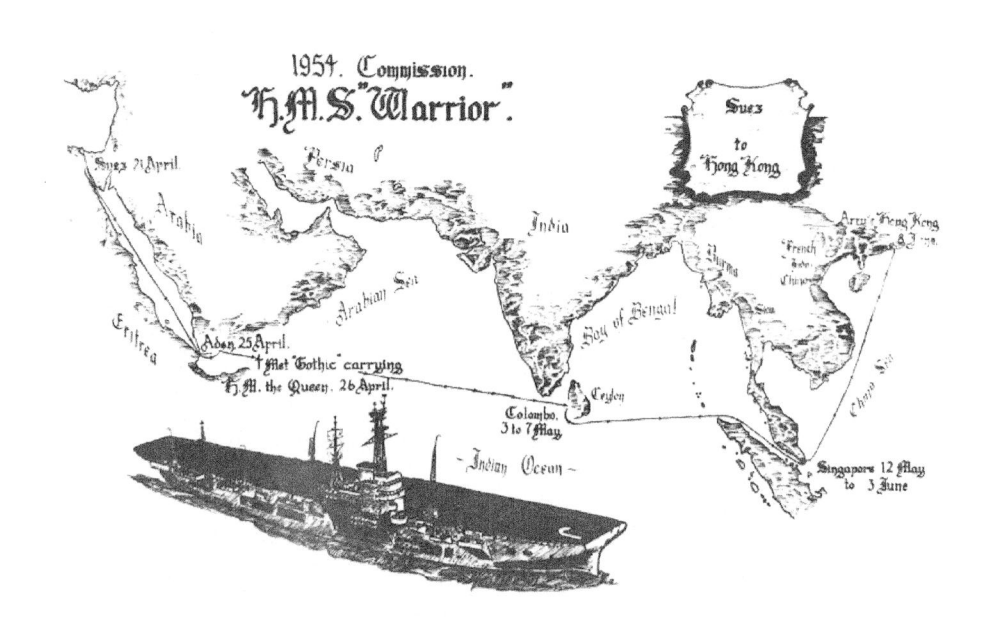

◆ ◆ ◆

## Monday 26th April 1954

Got up at 0400 this morning from 0430 to 0500 lookout, secured at 0600.

Our squadrons flew off at 1045 to fly past the "Gothic" which was some 100 miles away.

The hands cleaned into No. 6s at 1600 in preparation for meeting the Queen. The Gothic came into view at 1630 with an escort of a cruiser, HMS "Newfoundland" and 3 Pakistan destroyers.

We fired a 21 gun salute to HM the Queen and cruised alongside Gothic to give three cheers.

Her Majesty sent a signal saying we looked very smart and to **splice the mainbrace.**

*Note: Splice the Mainbrace - an order given onboard naval vessels to issue the crew with an alcoholic drink.*

*HMS Warrior alongside Gothic*

LESLIE EDWARD SMITH

This is an excerpt from Ray's website about this event:

*"In March 2005, Len Hillier sent the following about the day: On Monday 26th April 1954, the Liner Gothic (with HM The Queen onboard) escorted by HMS Newfoundland and three Pakistan frigates was on its way to Aden from a tour of Australia and New Zealand. Both our squadrons did a low level fly pass at 200 feet. Later on after landing the squadron back on board, we turned and overtook the Gothic and steamed past at 200yds. The lower deck was cleared with every possible man was on deck, nearly a thousand men fell in three deep all round the flight deck with the Royal Marine band in the bows, we could see HM the Queen and the Duke of Edinburgh, three mighty cheers rang out, and the signal flags for "long live the queen" were hoisted. Warrior steamed ahead to part company. A few minutes later a radio message was received "Thank you for your message. You looked very smart. Best wish for a happy commission." Soon after, we received the instruction to "Splice the Mainbrace", an issue of extra rum/grog (watered down rum)."*

### Tuesday 27th April 1954

The weather today has still been very warm, but the temperature below decks has dropped slightly.

We have been passing a series of Islands all day on the Port side and at 1100 this morning we passed the Eastern tip of Italian Somaliland.

At 1600 the ship entered absolute flat calm water.

Clocks are being forwarded 1/2 hour tonight.

I have got the last two hours of the first watch.

### Wednesday 28th April 1954

We are now in the Arabian Sea and the sea is flat calm.

Closed up for a shoot on the Bofors, the target was a balloon which on being released was shot down in the first run.

Started to paint the RPOs mess today, it was a grim job with the temperature in there 94 degrees and boy did I sweat.

I have the middle watch tonight, roll on Colombo let's get a run ashore.

### Thursday 29th April 1954

Very tired this morning after the middle watch.

Continued painting the RPOs mess.

Exercised boarding parties at 1030, we done firings on the Lanchester, our target being a bottle which we were touring ourselves.

Got my head down on the FX this afternoon and slept till 1700.

The weather today has been very warm with hardly any breeze.

I went to the pictures this evening on the flight deck, the film was "Three Little Words".

I have the morning watch.

### Friday 30th April 1954

Up at 0400 this morning, had a lookout from 0500 to 0530, weather very close with absolutely no breeze at all. Secured at 0600.

We worked Saturday routine today, messdeck rounds.

The ship at present is approx 180 miles from India but we are not going into harbour as we have more flying trials to do. It is expected that we shall enter Colombo harbour some time on Monday.

I have all night in my hammock tonight, good oh!

### Saturday 1st May 1954

There was quite a heavy storm last night and the sea this morning rather rough.

Ceylon was in sight at 0900 this morning off the Port Bow.

Continued with flying programme at 1300 flying off both squadrons. We had one crash on deck but there were no casualties. Secured from flying stations at 16.30.

The FA Cup final was played today between WBA and PNE being won by WBA by 3-2, the goals were scored by ALLEN 2 NICHOLS 1

### Sunday 2 May 1954

No divisions today the hands secured at 0945.

Went to flying stations at 1100 our aircraft doing dive bombing practice on a splash target, secured from flying stations at 1300.

The Captain addressed the ship's company on the flight deck at 1630 and told us our routine regarding Colombo and Singapore, he also told us the ship would be visiting Sasebo (Japan) during the tour of the Far East.

The sea today has been rather choppy and dull, with lightening at frequent intervals off the port side.

### Monday 3rd May 1954

Arrived at Colombo at 0900 securing to stern buoy and both anchors down ford.

Changed £1:17:6d into Rupees and caught the 1930 boat ashore, had one drink in the **NAAFI** with Evans. We met Seager and Dillon in there and went round the native quarters.

We bought a large bottle of the local gin and got very drunk. Evans and I lost Seager and Dillon so we went to the Salvation Army hotel where we slept the night.

*Note:* NAAFI - Navy, Army and Air Force Institute.

### Tuesday 4th May 1954

Got up feeling very rough this morning.

Caught the 0700 board back to the ship.

I haven't done any work today, feeling grim. I slept on the FX this afternoon but still wasn't myself when I woke.

I bought a set of Elephants today for 7/6d.

It has rained very hard all day today.

### Wednesday 5th May 1954

Half of the ship's company went on a day's trip to the ancient capital of Ceylon which is called **"Kandy"**.

Things today have been rather quiet onboard with the hands having a general make and mend.

There has not been any mail brought to the ship today as the comet jet airlines have been banned from flying owing to recent crashes.

We have been informed that we are to join up with the American 95th Task Force on our arrival in the Far East.

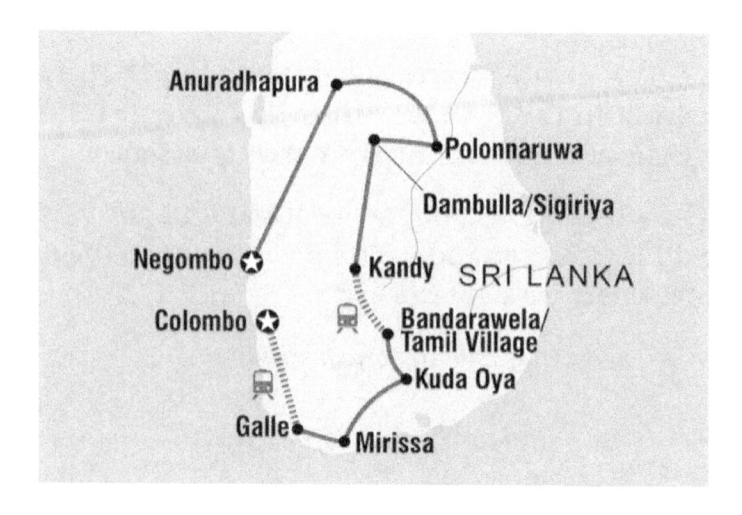

**Note:** *The ancient city of Kandy lies in the midst of the hills of the Kandy plateau which crosses an area of tropical plantations - mainly tea. I remember my father telling me one of the highlights of his visit to Sri Lanka was to be given a trip up into the hills of the Kandy plateau, he found it very moving.*

## Thursday 6th May 1954

The second half of the ship's company went to "Kandy" for the day.

Barbara's birthday today and I haven't even sent her a card, I bet she is fed up!!

There was a general make and mend for the remainder of the ship's company this afternoon.

I weighed myself today and found that I have lost 10lb, if I sweat anymore there will be nothing left of me.

The ship is expecting to leave Colombo at 1000 tomorrow.

I laid my kit out today all was well except No 6s badges.

# SRI LANKA TO SINGAPORE

*"How in all time of our distress,
As in our triumph too,
The game is more than the player of the game
And the ship is more than the crew!"*

*Rudyard Kipling*

◆ ◆ ◆

### Friday 7th May 1954

The ship left Colombo at 1000 this morning.

Mail came onboard just before we slipped. I had a letter from Barbara.

We went to flying stations on leaving harbour but secured just after twelve owning to weather conditions.

The ship's company got paid in the hangar at 1515 I got paid £5.

There is a guard regiment for General Templer Governor of Malaya so I volunteered today.

**Note:** *I thought it would be interesting to have a comparison of what £5 in today's money would be worth - at the time of writing (2020) it's would be worth about £135 ....so not a lot!*

### Saturday 8th May 1954

We worked a normal Saturday routine today, with Captain's messdeck rounds at 1000.

There was no flying carried out today.

I slept on the FX this afternoon where there was a very cool breeze blowing, the heat below deck is unbearable.

The clocks are being advanced 1/2 hour at 2345.

### Sunday 9th May 1954

There was morning service held onboard this morning at 0930.

The weather has been very warm today with the temperature in the messdecks reaching 96 degrees.

The clocks are to be advanced 1/2 hour again tonight.

Wrote a letter to Barbara this evening. I also have the first watch.

### Monday 10th May 1954

The hands went to flying stations at 0830, we flew off both squadrons using **R.A.T.O.G.** method flying continued until 1400.

The volunteers for the guard were assembled on the flight deck where we were measured and exercised marching.

The ship is now some 200 miles off Sumatra and the weather getting warmer.

The temperature in the mess today was 97 degrees.

Interpart (?) hockey was played on the flight deck this evening.

The clocks are to be advanced 1/2 hour at 1145 middle watchman closing up at time which is me!!!

*Note:* RATOG refers to "rocket assisted take-off gear"

### Tuesday 11th May 1954

Closed up for saluting gun drill at 0900.

Fired the Bofor guns at smoke target.

We passed an island at 1100 which is said to be infected with rats.

Went to the pictures this evening to see "The Card" which was a very good film.

Clocks are being advanced 1/2 hour tonight. I have the morning watch.

### Wednesday 12 May 1954

The ship entered the Jahore Strait at 0800 where we took onboard a pilot.

We arrived in Singapore dockyard at 1600 and went alongside.

I caught the first boat ashore with "Brum" Seager and we went into Singapore City calling at the Britannia Club for a drink where we also had big eats.

I bought a coffee set and a big box. I also bought a set of underwear for Barbara.

Singapore is a very nice place with plenty of entertainment.

We caught the 2330 boat back to the ship and was I tired.

### Thursday 13th May 1954

The weather today has been very warm with occasional showers.

We had all the Chinese traders onboard and our FX looked like the shopping centre of the world, and anything at all could be bought.

The Captain addressed the ship's company at 1600 regarding our future programme.

Our **libertymen** were sent back to the ship today owing to riot which were taking place ashore.

*Note: Libertyman - a sailor having permission to go ashore*

## Friday 14th May 1954

Today has been rather dull with nothing very exciting happening.

Weather today has been very hot, with showers.

I received a letter with a map in from Mom tonight.

My name was entered on the list for the Kuala Lumpur Guard today, we go for drill tomorrow.

## Saturday 15th May 1954

Messdeck rounds were not carried out today the Captain did upper deck rounds.

I lent out 20 Dollars until next pay day leaving myself with $22 so I went ashore with Evans and Taffy. First of all we had big eats, then a couple of beers after which we all went and got tattooed on our legs costing us $4, then we had a few more beers and got merry, we all shied up in a dance and got in with some English women. We have arranged to bring the women onboard tomorrow.

Caught a taxi back to the ship.

*Note: The tattoo my father had on his leg (on his outer calf - on his left leg as I remember) was a dragon. I so wish I had a photo of it now! It faded over the years, but I remember it well as a child and often asked to see it.*

## Sunday 16th May 1954

The hands went to divisions at 0900 dress No 6s, I did not attend.

Me and the lads won't be able to meet those women as we have not even got our bus fare?  Instead I got my head down until 1730.  I had a real good sleep.

Wrote a letter to Barbara this evening.

The ship is expected to go into the K.G. VI dock tomorrow morning, and half of the ship's company may go into HMS **"Terror"**.

*Note: My father stayed on HMS Terror while he was training for Guard Drill.*

## Monday 17th May 1954

The ship entered dry dock at 0900 and was docked down at approx 1500.

I packed my **case** and went into HMS "Terror" arriving at 1500.

I made my bed down and had tea, then I went to the MAA's Mess where I stayed till 2000 having a few bottles of **"Tiger"** and a "Tot" of neaters.

Went to the beer bar after with Evans, Tilley, and "Mick" Mills where we had a couple more beers, it was good oh.

*Note:  Tiger is a brand of beer from Singapore.*

*I assume the case which my father packed to stay onboard HMS Terror is the one issued to him by the navy - a brown one.  My sister still has this case (in which she keeps her Christmas decorations).  Here are some photos of it:*

*Below: The case was stamped with his initials L S*

## Tuesday 18th May 1954

Up at 0600 this morning. Went and shook the "Jaunty" at 0630. Had my breakfast in the "jauntys" mess (Big Eats).

Caught the bus back to the ship at 0710 to do parade training for the Kuala Lumpur guard.

Commenced drill at 0745 and secured at 0830, all went well.

I walked back into "Terror" after drill.

I haven't done a thing all day. This certainly is a quiet number?

### Wednesday 19th May 1954

Caught the bus back to the ship at 0710.

Commenced parade training at 0745 until 0830 after which I went back to "Terror".

On arriving back in "Terror" I helped to shear up the jaunty's mess.

Got my head down at 1300 until tea time and did I have a smashing sleep!!

I went to the beer bar on the night where I met "Brum" Seager - he bought me a pint of beer. Then we went to the pictures.

### Thursday 20th May 1954

Went onboard for parade training at 0710. We had a strenuous hour's drill which we did in dull but very clammy weather.

Arrived back in "Terror" at 0930 with nothing at all to do (what a life)!

Got my head down at 1300 until 1500 then I went for a game of snooker good oh.

Went to the pictures again this evening spending my last 50 cents. Roll on tomorrow, let's get some money.

Half of the ship's company went for Xrays today.

### Friday 21st May 1954

Went onboard for parade training at 0710. We did marching to the ship band, I found today's training rather enjoyable.

Came back to "Terror" for a couple of hours, then I went back onboard for payment. I was paid $45 so I decided to have a run ashore with the lads. We caught the 1400 bus into Nee Soon and had a smashing run!

I bought an American style jacket for $10 and am very pleased with it.

Arrived back onboard at 1230 feeling very tired.

What a day this has been?

### Saturday 22 May 1954

Continued parade training onboard this morning there was not much co-operation from the lads after our hectic runs ashore last night (Pay Night).

Arrived back at "Terror" at 0915 the loafed about the lamp? until **Up Spirits** then I went for dinner. Turned in for the afternoon and had a smashing sleep, got up at 1600.

Went to the beer bar at 1900 and had a few "Tigers".

*Note:* Up Spirits - this is a Boatswain's call for a Tot of rum. (The daily issue of rum was stopped in the Royal Navy in 1970)

### Sunday 23 May 1954

Got up at 0730 and went to breakfast with the lads.

Went for a game of cricket after breakfast, what a skylark we had! Packed up cricket at "Tot" time, had our rum and went in the beer bar, had a few pints on top of our rum and got rather drunk. We had our dinner then crashed.

Got up at 1630 feeling on top of the world, went to the Canteen at 1900 and had a very nice time.

## Monday 24th May 1954

Continued parade training, but the lads were not very enthusiastic after their hectic weekend.

I went back to "Terror" to pack my kit ready to join the ship again.

Wrote a letter to Barbara this morning.

Caught the bus back to the ship at 1330, I would like to have stopped in "Terror" a little longer as I enjoyed myself very much.

Slung my hammock on FX which was very uncomfortable as the dockyard workmen have been working there.

## Tuesday 25th May 1954

Parade training was resumed today with our drill being a little better. There may be a full dress rehearsal tomorrow.

Had a very quiet forenoon onboard, I finished my work by 1030.

Went down the dock bottom this afternoon to see how the dockyard are progressing with our bottom. Things seem to be going quite well.

I got $20 paid back to me today which was owning to me. It will come in very handy for Kuala Lumpur.

## Wednesday 26th May 1954

Continued with parade training for the guard so far so good.

Had a very quiet day today with hardly anything to do.

The ship is expected to undock on Saturday morning.

The Australian Aircraft Carrier "Sydney" left Singapore for Australia today. "Warrior" is the "Sydney's" relief.

LESLIE EDWARD SMITH

### *Thursday 27th May 1954*

We carried out a full dress rehearsal for the Guard this morning in very hot weather. We were inspected by the Commodore of the dockyard, one of our lads flaked out.

Had our No 6 suits inspected ready for Saturday.

The weather today has been grim with the temperature reaching 96 degrees. Roll on UK.

I received two letters today one from Barbara with a map in it and one from Bill, also with a couple of maps in, very pleased.

### *Friday 28th May 1954*

There was not much to our Guard drill this morning, as we had a briefing on our routine as regards to us going to Kuala Lumpur tomorrow.

The ship's bottom was completed this forenoon, so the dock was flooded at 1300.

Packed my gear ready for tomorrow and cleaned up my webbing equipment.

I bought a civvy shirt costing me $5 as we are allowed to wear civvies in K.L.

### *Saturday 29th May 1954*

The ship undocked at 0800 this morning.

The K.L. guard caught the 0910 train from Jahore Bahru station, having a 240 mile journey ahead of us.

Our journey was rather uncomfortable as the weather was very warm. We arrived in Kuala Lumpur at 1930.

We were then taken by Army lorries to a transit camp and what a place this was.

We drew our bedding, and went for supper which was a small portion of stew, boy did our bowls drip.

*Note:* *Drips - naval slang for continual grumbling.*

### Sunday 30th May 1954

Up at 0700 and went for breakfast which was kippers, more drips!!

Mustered in our equipment at 0830 ready for a rehearsal at Pho airport where we were taken by lorries being greeted on arrival by the Somerset Regt and the Malay police.

We all marched on to the air strip and did a 2 hour drill, it was grim. We did the same thing at 1700 and was the lads "chocker".

I went ashore in civvies and had a very good run.

### Monday 31st May 1954

Feeling rather groggy after my run ashore last night.

We all cleared into No 6s at 0800 and set out for the air strip. The Navy was the first to arrive. We marched on at 0900. The Guard of Honour was provided by the Malayan airforce. General Templer arrived after the 9 Malay rulers and inspected the parade.

We took off from the airfield at approx 1000. Was I glad to get out of that sun. We were the only guard not to have a man faint.

Toured a Tin mine this afternoon. Caught the 2000 train back to Singapore.

### Tuesday 1st June 1954

Had a hectic journey back arriving in Jahore Barhu at 0900 taking us 13 hours in all. Got back to the ship at 0915. I had a smashing shower when I got back onboard and breakfast, there was also a letter from Mom waiting for me.

The ship weighed and proceeded at 1500 to Singapore Roads and dropped anchor.

There was a free cinema show on the flight deck so I went with "Brum" Seager.

## Wednesday 2nd June 1954

Weighed anchor ay 0630 and proceeded to fly on our squadrons.

The sky was very heavy this morning and it rained very hard for a couple of hours.

All our aircraft had flown on by 1600 without any crashes.

The ship proceeded back to Singapore Roads and the anchor was dropped at 1930.

I had my hair cut ready for payment tomorrow.*

***Note** - the Pay Parades were used to inspect a ratings appearance.

## Thursday 3rd June 1954

Weighed and proceeded at 0630 to commence flying trials.

Closed up for drill on the Saluting guns for 30 minutes.

The ship anchored in Singapore Roads at 1430 to embark "AVGAS". I was lined up for being absent from place of duty namely the Saluting Gun Crew, as we saluted the flag at the C.in C. (17 guns) I was placed in the Commander's report, am I fed up?

Lower deck was cleared at 1515 for payment, I drew $55.

There was no "AVGAS" available for us so we got underway for Hong Kong at 1730.

I have the middle watch tonight.

# SINGAPORE TO HONG KONG

*"Swiftly, swiftly flew the ship,*
*Yet she sailed softly too:*
*Sweetly, sweetly blew the breeze—*
*On me alone it blew."*

Samuel Taylor Coleridge

◆ ◆ ◆

### Friday 4th June 1954

Felt a little tired after my middle watch, roll on Hong Kong.

Saw the Commander this morning he gave me 3 days No. 14 which equals 2 hours extra work at night.

We commenced to fly off our aircraft at 0900.

I got my head down until 1430 after which Gun Aimers were briefed on control orders which included me.

Mustered at 1700 for work, I had to hump all scram bag gear on to the FX and back. I have never been so chocker in all my life.

The temperature reached over 100 degrees in our mess today.

### Saturday 5th June 1954

The Commander did messdeck rounds today.

Commenced flying at 0900. Slept on the FX this afternoon and there was a wonderful breeze flowing. The last of our aircraft landed on at 1600.

Fell in for punishment at 1700 and got detailed for the same job as I did last night (humping scram bag gear onto the FX).

We ran into some very heavy showers this evening but I did not mind as they helped to cool the ship down a little.

Have all night in my hammock, good oh.

## Sunday 6th June 1954

I didn't get up until 0730 this morning. I had an argument with the RPOs, am chocker. Went down and saw the Chief G.I. for a change of jobs.

The Captain did upper deck rounds at 0930.

Slept on the FX this afternoon and there was a wonderful breeze blowing.

The Captain addressed the ship's company on our routine when we arrive in Japan.

I have the first watch tonight, roll on Hong Kong.

Changed my Singapore money to Hong Kong. I have 84 Hong Kong $.

## Monday 7th June 1954

We commenced flying at 0715 getting off both of our squadrons.

There was a minor accident when one of our aircraft made a bad landing, there were no casualties.

I slept on the FX all afternoon.

Secured from flying at 1600. I wrote letter to Mom and Barbara this evening. The temperature below decks at 1600 was 100 degrees.

The ship is expected to arrive at Hong Kong at approx 0800 tomorrow morning.

I have the middle watch tonight.

## Tuesday 8th June 1954

We arrived at Hong Kong at 0800 and tied up alongside the fuelling wharf.

We went further into the harbour on completion of embarking "AVGAS". An 11 Gun Salute was fired for the C. in C.

I went ashore at 1700 with Evans and Taffy calling in the China Fleet Club where we had 2 **John Collins**. We then went to the Shanghai Hotel where we stayed all evening, and oh what a night we had, Evans proposed to a Chinese girl!!

I stayed ashore all night.

**Note:** *John Collins is a Cocktail. I never knew my father ever to drink cocktails but he obviously enjoyed them during his navy days.*

## Wednesday 9th June 1954

Got up at 0600 this morning feeling a little rough after last night. Got onboard at 0700.

The hands were employed in ammunitioning taking onboard bombs and rockets.

The amount of work I have done today is practically nil? I slept all afternoon on the FX as I was feeling very tired after my run ashore.

Went to the pictures this evening with Taffy and "Mick" Mills and it was quite a good show.

### Thursday 10th June 1954

Ammunitioning was continued today taking onboard Rockets and Bombs etc. Today being the Birthday of H.M. The Queen a 21 Gun Salute was fired by "Warrior", "Tamar" and the Army. A make and mend was given to the Port watch with leave.

I went ashore at 1700 with Evans, going first to Kowloon where we spent a couple of hours in the NAAFI after which we went by Ferry to Hong Kong. We had a good time in a dance hall which is called the "LIDO" where to get a dance one had to buy a ticket.

Evans and I had big eats (fried prawns), we slept onshore.

### Friday 11th June 1954

Up at 0600 and it was absolutely pouring with rain. Evans and I decided to have breakfast in the China Fleet Club which I enjoyed very much. We caught the 0700 boat and got drowned going back to the ship.

Had a very quiet day onboard with not much work to do?

I slept all afternoon on the FX, was I tired after last night !!!

The ship is expected to get underway for Japan tomorrow.

DIARY OF AN ABLE SEAMAN - 1954

# HONG KONG TO JAPAN

*"I must go down to the seas again, for
the call of the running tide
Is a wild call and a clear call that may not be denied"*

(John Masefield)

◆ ◆ ◆

### *Saturday 12th June 1954*

The ship left Hong Kong at 0900 for Kobe (Japan).

The weather today has been very cool and the sea was calm.

I slept all afternoon on the FX and I did not wake until 1640 so the R.P.O.s got no tea!!!

I have the morning watch, what a way to spend a weekend?

### *Sunday 13th June 1954*

I was up at 0400 this morning being detailed as sea boats crew. The sea boat was exercised away at 0630 after which I secured.

It has been a very quiet day with most of the ship's company sleeping on the upper deck.

My watch has the last dog, and all night in tonight.

I am coming off R.P.O.s messmen tomorrow and am I glad.

### Monday 14th June 1954

Changed my job today to After flat Sweeper. I was put in the **rattle** sohie(?)* 15 minutes after taking over my new post. Saw the O.O.W (Mr Ulpett ) he gave me a Commander's report, am I "chocker".

Commenced flying at 0630 and secured at 1100 owing to bad visibility. Passed Okinowa class of island at 1100 which has been volcanic since 1901, it was to rear starboard. The ship should be off Formosa some time tomorrow.

We entered a gale at 1500 with a very severe wind blowing, visibility was only up to a few yards.

Done some aiming practice.

*Note: "Rattle" seems some kind of naval slang for punishment:*
*"Having committed an offence and being placed in the Captain's or Commander's report, a naval rating will say that he is "in the rattle" or he has "scored a rattle" - possibly from the meaning of the word rattle, "to rail at in a noisy manner", as a defaulter supposes the Captain or Commander will do.*

*Photo of illegible word:

### Tuesday 15th June 1954

I was up at 0400 this morning and there was a very strong wind blowing. I scrabbled the compass platform at 0530 and secured from sea boat crew at 0645.

We commenced to fly off aircraft at 0700. I got settled into my new job today and worked pretty hard.

Saw the Commander at 1500, he gave me 5 days **No** 10s which meant I have practically no time to myself. "Am I cheesed off".

I had the afternoon watch abreast the sea boat, I also have the middle watch. Roll on my seven.

*Notes: No. 10s naval punishment seems to have been in numbers.*
*No 9s stoppage of leave, pay and Tot.*
*No10s, stoppage of leave.*
*No14s two hours extra work*
*There was also second class for conduct.*

## Wednesday 16th June 1954

Turned to on the FX at 0730 and scrubbed down. The ship anchored off Kobe at 0800 where we met HMS Defender and supplied her with stores. (No leave was given).

I had a make and mend because I kept the middle watch last night.

I did 1 hours doubling on the flight deck from 0700 until 1800 then I worked up to 2045. I have never been so thread bare in all my life. I have also got the morning watch on top of this lot.

I should have written to Barbara this evening but I just haven't the time.

Payday today, I picked up £5=0=0.

## Wednesday 17th June 1954

We weighed anchor and proceeded for "Kure" at 0145.

I was up at 0400 for the morning watch. I secured at 0800. Turned to at 0900 for General drill on the flight deck. We rigged light **Jackstay** for 1hr replenishment of a Destroyer at sea. This was completed at 1030.

I worked in the Galley for my dinner hour punishment.

The ship entered Kure harbour at 1400 and we tied up alongside the **"Empire Fowey"**. Half of the ship's company went onshore, I was employed polishing **brightwork?**

**Notes** - *A Jackstay is used for transferring personnel, provisions, and light stores.*

*Brightwork refers to the exposed and varnished wood or metal work of a boat or ship.*

*Empire Fowey was a troopship.*

## Friday 18th June 1954

I was detailed for storing Party and what a job too, we got onboard 130 bags of spuds, I got rather sunburnt doing it.

During the dinner hour I worked in the Galley shelling peas. Went to quarters, clean guns at 1330 till 1400 then back to store ship.

I doubled from 1700 to 1800 on the flight deck with a rifle and was I warm, we had to wear long blue trousers which weren't helping any. Worked right up till 2100. This punishment gets me down.

We had mail onboard today and I never had a letter.

## Saturday 19th June 1954

We moved berth at 0830, going further out into the harbour and tying to a buoy.

It rained pretty hard this morning.

I worked in the Galley all afternoon washing up greasy trays. What a job!!! Roll on tomorrow and let's get off punishment.

I am also duty watch being detailed as Emergency party. This ship is expecting to get underway for Sasebo at 0400 in the morning.

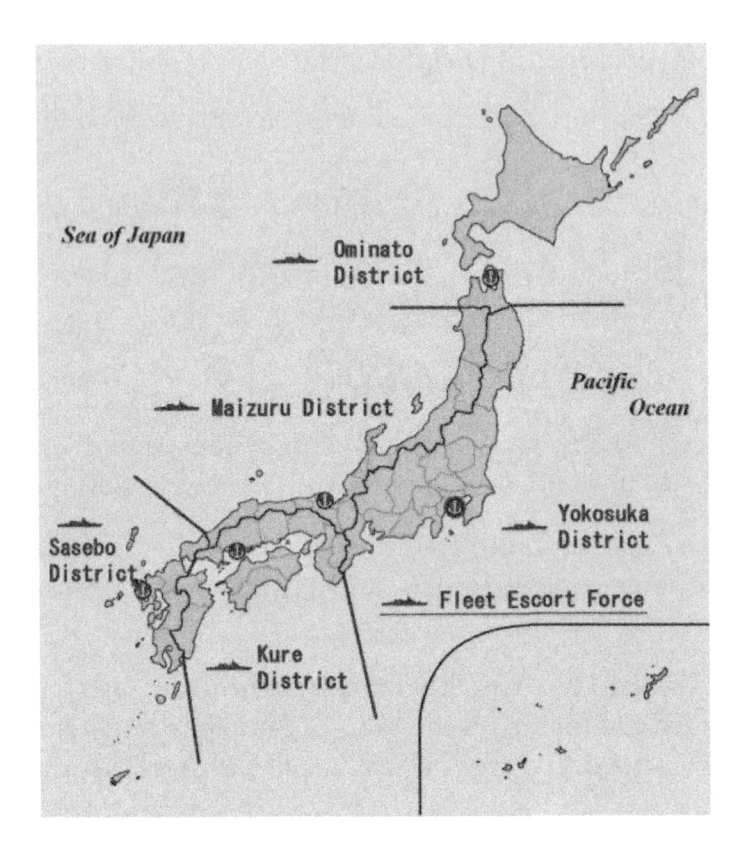

*JAPAN: Kure to Sasebo*

## Sunday 20th June 1954

The port watch was called at 0330 to get the ship to sea. We were underway at approx 0430. There was a very strong wind blowing so we secured everything for sea.

I did my last muster for punishment at 1300, was I glad?

I slept all afternoon and woke at 1600, I mustered for the 1st

Dog. I did lookout from 1700-1800 because this area is mined.

I mustered with my part of the watch at 2000 to clear up messdecks and flats.

E.T.A. tomorrow at 0630.

**Note:** *E.T.A. - Estimated Time of Arrival*

## *Monday 21st June 1954*

Up at 0330 this morning, morning watchman. Prepared the starboard Ford ladder for lowering.

The ship arrived in Sasebo harbour at 0630 and we secured with a simple bridle ford. The American aircraft carrier "Wright" was at anchor when we arrived.

I did plenty of work today vacuuming the whole of my flat?

There is no mail in Sasebo for "Warrior", it has been almost 4 days since we had any now.

## *Tuesday 22nd June 1954*

We put to sea at 0945 in company with the U.S.S. "Wright", 2 American and 2 Canadian destroyers.

I closed up action lookout at 1100 for 1 hour, there was a very strong wind blowing.

Closed up at action stations at 1430 for 3/4 of an hour.

We darkened ship at 1900, I had the first watch doing 1 hour lookout form 2200-2300 and it was very windy and rough. The ship had a pretty steep roll on.

We remained following in line ahead of "Wright" through the night.

### Wednesday 23rd June 1954

The sea is still a little choppy but not as bad as last night. The port watch went to defence stations at 1030 where we remained until 1130.

I had afternoon watch and closed up in the wheelhouse until 1330 after which the hands closed up at action stations.

Both our squadrons and the "Wright" squadron were flown off at 1400, they exercised attack on the ships.

Secured from actions stations at 1300.

I have the middle watch tonight.

### Thursday 24th June 1954

Carried out exercises with ships in company all forenoon, also had lookouts closed up searching for mines.

I had a make and mend this afternoon (Middle watchman). Gun crews closed up for tracking exercise at 1330 but I was excused. Had the first dog in the wheelhouse, did a 40 minutes trick on the wheel.

Closed up messdecks at 2000 for rounds, then I went to the pictures with "Brum" Seager, the film was **"The Red Boat"**. I have the morning watch.

*Note: I cannot find details of a film called "The Red Boat". My father may have got the title wrong.*

### Friday 25th June 1954

Up at 0400 this morning, went on lookout until 0500 and was it cold, I was froze.

Secured at 0800 and went to breakfast. Falling in again at 0900 the amount of work I did this morning was NIL.

Both of our squadrons were flown off at 1400 so were U.S.S. "Wright's" aircraft. All gun crews were closed up and we fired break up shot at our own aircraft which were attacking the ship, all went well.

We had 6 bags of mail bought onboard by helicopter, I had two letters.

I have the last day and all night in.

*HUP2 Retriever from USS Wright bring mail to HMS Warrior*

## Saturday 26th June 1954

Prepared gear ready for fuelling Canadian destroyers which came alongside at 0900. Our first attempt was unsuccessful as our oil line parted causing great panic onboard "Warrior". There were a couple of Canadians with minor injuries.

Commenced fuelling again at 1200 with both watches of seamen working up till 1800 and there were plenty of drips from the lads.

U.S.S. "Wright" fuelled the American destroyer, and done it in much faster time than we.

I have first watch tonight, I won't be sorry when we get in harbour.

Fuelling - Warrior 1953

## Sunday 27th June 1954

This forenoon has been very quiet (there were no divisions) at 1200 the Captain of U.S.S. "Wright" came onboard.

I closed up at 1230 for the afternoon watch, we had to put up darken ship screens in preparation for exercises. I did one and half hours in the wheelhouse.

The ship was darkened at approx 2000. I have got the middle watch and we are closing up at dawn action stations. It looks as though I ain't going to get any sleep for 24 hours.

## Monday 28th June 1954

I had middle watch, and the hands went to action stations at 0410 meaning I had the morning too. Both our squadrons were flown off at 0530 so were the U.S.S. "Wright's". We were attacked by American sabre jets all through the forenoon. We went into defence stations at 0800. I kept the forenoon and did I feel tired. Secured at 1230 and got my head down, did I need it. I was up at

1600, I had the first dog. We parted company with U.S.S. Wright and the escorting destroyers at 1630, they carried on to Japan, and we sailed for Inchon (Korea)

I have the morning watch.

### Tuesday 29th June 1954

Up at 0400, was detailed as O.O.W. messenger. It was absolutely pouring with rain when I went on watch and visibility was down to roughly 30 yards. I was kept very busy by the O.O.W. who was the 1st Lieut.

We met "Wave Preview" at 0530 and went alongside for fuel but the weather was not suitable, so we abandoned the task until 0900, this time we managed to commence embarking our fuel. Fuelling was completed by 1400 after which the hands secured (I got my head down).

The ship dropped anchor at 1530 in shallow water, getting underway again at 1800. I was lookout for mines on the flight deck for 1 hour. We anchored again at 2000.

### Wednesday 30th June 1954

The anchor was weighed and we proceeded to Inchon at 0415 arriving at 0715.

A make and mend was given to the Port watch which was me so I spent it resting!!

Today I am cook of the mess, how I hate the job.

Had a game of deck hockey this evening and did I get battered, I can hardly walk.

Leave was given today to a limited number of men, I did not bother to put my name forward.

## Thursday 1 July 1954

Prepared the **flat** for painting tonight up to 1030 then I closed up for aiming practice on the S.T.D.

The ship's company went to general payment at 1130 on the Flight deck. I picked up £5=0=0.

A make and mend was given to the starboard watch with leave. I took one too?

I am duty watch tonight but I haven't anything special to do.

Turned to at 2200 painting the deck in the after flat, finished at 0045.

*Note: Flat - open space between mess decks onboard ship.*

## Friday 2nd July 1954

Captain's messdeck rounds at 1030 all went well.

The ship got underway for Kure in company with the two American destroyers.

I had a make and mend because I worked last night. I had the first dog, went up the wheelhouse, did one hour on the wheel.

Cleared up messdecks and flats.

The miles we have steamed since leaving UK were given today.

19,200 miles have been steamed and 83 out of 134 days spent at sea.

## Saturday 3rd July 1954

We were to fly off our squadrons this forenoon but owning to bad weather it was not possible. A gunnery exercise was also cancelled, break up shot was to be fired.

I slept from 1330 until 1600.

Had the last dog bridge messenger, was rather boring.

Today has been pretty quiet onboard. The U.S.S. "Phillip" and "Renshaw" remained in company with us.

### Sunday 4th July 1954

Helped to rig the church at 0800 (watch on deck). I was lookout from 0930 - 1030, and the weather is grim with the visibility very poor.

Got my head down during the afternoon, there was nothing else to do.

Both watches of the hands fell in at 1830 and prepared for entering Kure. It was absolutely pouring with rain. The ship secured in our old berth (alongside).

Went ashore at 2045 with Evans, Tolley and Searth and oh what a night we had. We decided to stay ashore the night seeing we had all night leave.

### Monday 5th July 1954

Felt rather tired this morning, I was awake by 0500. Was back onboard by 0645.

We had a new First Lieutenant take over today. Lt. Cdr. Lamb leaves the ship on Wednesday.

I received a letter from Barbara when I got onboard, I was quite pleased. Got my head down in the hammock netting this afternoon where no-one could see me?

Duty watch tonight, I am emergency party.

It was very quiet in the mess tonight as most of the lads are ashore.

## Tuesday 6th July 1954

It has been a very quiet day onboard, with not very much exciting happening.

Went ashore at 1700 with Evans & Tolley, first we went buying presents. Then we took our buy to the KURE Azure for safe keeping, then we went to town and oh what a night we had? We clued up in "Betty's Bar" where we stayed until they were closed. We all stayed ashore tonight.

*On this day my father had a pencil drawing done in Kure, Japan. (I felt quite emotional when I saw this drawing after many years: that someone had drawn so intimately my father's features to a very good likeness).*

### Wednesday 7th July 1954

Felt a bit rough when I woke up this morning, caught a taxi back to the ship arrive onboard at 0645.

Went to sick bay at 0800 with my eye, it feels grim.

Today I haven't done a stroke of work. I can't seem to find the energy for work after my runs ashore!!!

Had a very quiet evening onboard, and do I need it.

The troopship "Captain Hobson" left Kure at 1800 loaded with troops, she is bound for Liverpool.

### Thursday 8th July 1954

Had a pretty quiet forenoon with not much to do.

I was detailed to work with the side party during the afternoon. We painted the foot topping, from rafts. I got covered with paint? Decided to have a quiet run ashore with the lads, got ready and was ashore by 1945 went for a few drinks in the "Miss Kure" bar then we took a walk round in the end, we clued up in "Betty's Bar" where we got rather drunk.

Evans and Seager walked out on me leaving me on my own, I had to walk back to the ship, I had no Taxi fare to get back.

### Friday 9th July 1954

Was sent outside the Jaunty's office for slack hammock, the P.O. let me off.

I told Evans and Seager what I thought of the trick they played on me. The hands have been employed in sorting ship all day, I have been working in the flat but I didn't do much.

A rehearsal of the leading of the retreat was carried out on the flight deck at 1100, all went well. I am duty watch tonight, I am hammock stower.

The duty watch were employed in storing, we finished at 1800. I have been really chocker all day today.

### Saturday 10th July 1954

Captain's upper deck round at 1100, I caught the bus for Hiroshima at 1230 arriving at 1400. Hiroshima I found to be very interesting. I saw the spot where the "A" bomb actually exploded. I found the progress made in the re-building of the city was terrific.

The bus left at 1700 arriving back to the ship at 1800, I had my supper onboard then I went ashore.

I had a smashing time, met two M.P.s and got rather drunk, I stayed ashore all night.

### Sunday 11th July 1954

Got up at 0640 and was I tired, I only just got back onboard in time?

Divisions was held onboard at 0900 dress No. 6s, the Captain addressed the ship's company.

The troopship "Lancashire" came alongside at 1000, she was loaded with troops.

Each division had their photo taken on the flight deck for the ship's magazine.

I slept all afternoon on the cable deck, and did I need it.

### Monday 12th July 1954

Call the Port watch went at 0355 this morning which was me, we got the ship to sea. The Port watch secured at 0515.

Mustered for the forenoon watch and got detailed for a birch(?)* (Lookout) from 0900-1000.

I stayed on the upper deck nearly all afternoon, admiring the scenery.

The sea started to get a little choppy at 1700, we have a steady roll on and are going head on into it.

I have the first watch tonight.

* *Photo of illegible word:*

### Tuesday 13th July 1954

The sea was still rather choppy this morning, with a strong wind blowing.

I had the afternoon watch as O.O.W. Messenger.

Our flying programmes were cancelled today owing to the weather.

Went to the pictures this evening to see Cosh Boy which I enjoyed very much.

At 2000 the weather had deteriorated somewhat. The U.S.S. Philip has been out with us today.

### Wednesday 14th July 1954

The weather is much calmer today and we commenced flying. I was detailed as lookout from 1030-1130 during which time one of our aircraft crashed, the Pilot was OK.

I had a make and mend this afternoon, and slept like a log.

The ship anchored off Paran at 1500. At 1630 our helicopter crashed into the sea, the Pilot and observers were picked up with minor injuries.

Divers were out to locate the "Copter" but could not and the search was abandoned.

U.S.S. "Philip" anchored with us.

### Thursday 15th July 1954

Up at 0400 this morning, the ship got underway at 0500.

We commenced flying at 0800.

I am cook of the mess today, am I chocker.

I was lookout for 1 hour from 1340 - 1440. One of our "Firefly" was ditched into the sea, the Pilot and observer being picked up by a Yankee helicopter.

Flying was completed by 1700.

I had the last dog as O.O.W. messenger. I have all night in tonight, thank God.

*Fairey Firefly*

## Friday 16th July 1954

Commenced flying at 0730 this morning.

I had the forenoon watch, keeping part of it as O.O.W. messenger.

Our squadron took off loaded with 500lb bombs at 1400, we saw an exhibition bombing run by one of our "Fireflies"

Flying was completed by 1700 and the ship's company were paid on the flight deck. I drew £8=10=0

Mustered for the first watch, I had second hour lookout, it was a very clear night.

## Saturday 17th July 1954

Fell in at 0630 to oil ship from "Golden Ranger" (London) it was very windy and the sea choppy. I secured from oiling at 0900 and cleaned my flat ready for the 1st Lieut's inspection.

I had the afternoon and lookout from 1330-1430 it was raining very hard and the wind was at gale force. The American destroyer "Philip" was fuelling ahead of us from "Golden

Ranger". We had to turn in the sea boats as it was a little too rough. I got drownded in doing so. I have the middle watch tonight.

### Sunday 18th July 1954

The hands worked until 0900 then secure was piped.

Church service was held in the ford lift well. I slept all afternoon having kept the middle last night, I woke at 1845 and mustered for the first dog.

Got my fur-lined boots from the **snobs** this evening, they are very nice too, I still have one pound to pay on them.

Ordered a necklace set for Barbara from the canteen.

Cleared up the seaman hands for rounds. I have the morning watch.

*Note:* Snob - cobbler

LESLIE EDWARD SMITH

*HMS Warrior Cobbler*

## Monday 19th July 1954

Up at 0400 for the morning watch, it was a clammy camp morning.

I secured at 0700 and we had to close up for firings but it was cancelled owing to weather conditions.

Had to clear the DCHQ flat ready for spraying.

Closed up again at 1430 for firings. We engaged statshell (?) targets which were fired by a U.S. destroyer, the shoot went very well.

Closed up for the last dog, and was employed in re-packing **bofor** cylinders. I have all night in.

**Note:** *Bofor - artillery.*

## Tuesday 20th July 1954

Closed up for the forenoon watch. I did lookout for 1 hour from 0900-1000 during which time our squadron of "Furys" took off for **strafing** off "Okinowa". I also did lookout from 1200-1230. The two American destroyers came alongside for the transferring of Radar personnel, we also received mail from the U.S.S. "Philip", I had a letter from Barbara and was I pleased.

The Yanks lent us some films so I went to a free show tonight.

I have the first watch tonight.

The weather has been very warm today with the temperature reaching an average of 92 degrees.

**Note:** *Strafing is the military practice of attacking ground targets from low-flying aircraft using aircraft-mounted automatic weapons. Less commonly, the term is used by extension to describe high-speed firing runs by any land or naval craft such as fast boats, using smaller-caliber weapons and targeting stationary or slowly-moving targets*

## Wednesday 21st July 1954

Our squadrons were catapulted off for exercises on the Okinowa beaches.

I closed up for the afternoon watch at 1230, and was detailed as O.O.W.'s messenger from 1500-1600. It was raining very hard, and the visibility was down to approx 100 yards.

Fly was abandoned for the day at 1630.

I slung a clean hammock this evening, in preparation for Saturday's rounds.

I have the middle watch tonight, roll on Kure!!!

### Thursday 22nd July 1954

Had a pretty good middle, I slept most of the time.

Both our squadrons were flown off at 0700 for further exercise off "Okinowa".

I had a make and mend, and slept like a log.

At 1500 one of our "Fireflies" crashed in to the sea, the observer was picked up by an American destroyer, the Pilot was drowned. The Pilot was Lt Biles.

I kept the last dog. Personnel were returned to the Yankee destroyers at 1830.

I have the morning watch.

### Friday 23rd July 1954

Up at 0400 for the morning watch, I did my watch in the wheelhouse, doing a trick of 1 and a quarter hour, on the wheel.

Two American destroyers came alongside for flying programme.

Our squadrons were flown off for exercise this morning.

We parted company with the American destroyers at P.M.

I changed my money from B.A.F.K.s to YEN ready for Kure tomorrow!!

I kept the last dog, the ship at present is approx 33 miles off the Japanese coast, which is quite visible on the Port side.

### Saturday 24th July 1954

Had the forenoon watch, and was O.O.W. messenger.

A rehearsal of the beating of the retreat was held on the flight deck.

The commander did messdeck rounds.

We entered Kure harbour at 1800, in No 10s.

I went ashore with Dillon, we got rather drunk and decided to stay ashore the night. I had a wonderful time ashore.

## Sunday 25th July 1954

I woke up this morning feeling rather tired, I was bit all over with mosquitos. Returned onboard to find there was divisions in No 6s - was I chocker!!

There was church service held onboard for the late Lt. Biles.

I went ashore at 1400 for a walk round etc I had to get a sub first for duty post. I had big eats in Kure House in the afternoon with Newton. Met Seager and Dillon on the night and did we get drunk. I bought a 'Kimono'. There was a ship's concert at Kure House.

I slept ashore the night!! I lost my cap.

*Madam Harrison, Ship's concert, Kure, Japan, 1954*

*Ship's Concert, Kure, HMS Warrior, 1954*

*Navvy Jones, Ship's concert, Kure, Japan, 1954*

## Monday 26th July 1954

There was a terrific storm at 0300 this morning, I wondered what the hell was happening.

I woke up dead tired, Seager and I got a taxi back to the ship, we were 1/4 hour late but got away with it.

Admiral Gladstone, F.O.2 F.E.S. inspected "Warrior" below deck, he was quite pleased with what he found.

I took a make and mend, and slept all afternoon. Stayed onboard tonight and had a quiet evening.

## Tuesday 27th July 1954

I am storing party today spuds etc.

HMS Newfoundland left Kure at 1000.

I worked really hard today storing and the weather was very warm.

I went ashore with Evans, Whittle & Searth. We had a marvellous run, getting well oiled? We stayed in "Betty's Bar" all evening, dancing.

We were adrift returning to the ship and got lined up and oh what a skylark we had, we were given Commander's report.

## Wednesday 28th July 1954

I was up at 0400, the first watch got the ship to sea. I was feeling grim.

Saw the Cdr. at 0900 and he gave us Captain's report whom we saw at 1030, the Captain wasn't pleased and stopped me 14 days leave and 1 day's pay.

I kept the forenoon watch and was lookout from 1100 to 1230.

We exercised closing up aimers this morning.

We secured for sea at 1500, we are expecting rough weather.

I have the first watch tonight.

## ~ Interlude ~

*On this day it is recorded that a Sub-Lieutenant B J Magee of HMS Warrior, 845 Squadron, died from an illness, aged 20. My father makes no mention of this at all in his diary though he often records deaths and illnesses onboard ship, but this one is not written about - maybe he didn't know about it. There is a memorial plaque to B J Magee in Yokahama War Cemetery - date of death on the plaque recorded as 28th July 1954:*

Photograph by Michel Nelis. Used with Permission

*Then on 31 July 1954 there was a burial, but again my father makes no record of this event. I do not know why he makes no mention of it, because he records the deaths of Sub. Lt. Evans and Lt. Biles. Maybe the ratings did not get to hear of this death as it was due to an illness ~*

Yokohama, Japan. 31 July 1954. Burial of Sub-Lieutenant B. J. Magee, Royal Navy, HMS Warrior, at the British Commonwealth Cemetery in Yokohama. Note the guard of honour which has been formed and the Chaplain walks in front of the coffin.

## Thursday 29th July 1954

The sea is much calmer this morning.

The gun's crews were closed up at 0730 for a prize shoot but weather conditions did not permit.

We lowered our motor cutter which went over to an American destroyer, we took onboard 1 Officer and 1 P.O.

I mustered for pay at 1130 on the flight deck, I drew £5=0=0, finished paying for my boots.

Both our squadrons took off at 1330 whilst I was on lookout, the machine gunned a splash target.

I have the middle watch tonight.

### Friday 30th July 1954

Felt very tired after my middle. Commenced flying at 0800. It has been rather a quiet forenoon, I scrubbed paintwork.

I got my head down on the F.X. at 1300 and slept up till 1530. I mustered for the first dog at 1630, one of our "Furies" crashed the barriers, there were no casualties.

I closed up messdeck at 2030 for rounds.

There was a cinema show onboard but I did not go.

I have the morning watch.

### Saturday 31st July 1954

Up at 0400 feeling chocker. Was lookout from 0400-0700. At 0700 we commenced to take onboard "AVGAS" from "WAVE PREMIER". The Port watch secured at 0800 Starboard watch taking over the fuelling.

Turned to at 0900 "Wave Premier" was slipped at approx 1100.

I slept all afternoon. Mustered for the last dog, and at 1800 the American destroyer in company sighted a torpedo and picked it up. The fish was turned over to "Warrior", we believe it is Russian, and are keeping it for investigating.

The port of the watch rigged cinema.

**Note:** *This was the date of the burial of* Sub. Lt. B J Magee *referred to above, though my father makes no mention of it.*

## Sunday 1st August 1954

Closed up on the bridge, O.O.W. messenger until 1000. The American destroyer took stations ahead of us.

I secured at 1230, and got my head down for the afternoon. I woke at 1630 and went onto the flight deck where there was plenty of sport taking place, rifle shooting etc.

I closed up for the first watch and was lookout from 2000-2100, the evening was very cool. There were 3 cinema shows onboard tonight, I could not attend any.

At 2300 there was a rather strong wind blowing and the ship was rolling.

## Monday 2nd August 1954

The Port watch were **piped** to fall in at 0630, ammunition supply parties were detailed. Had a real good **loaf** this morning.

We lowered a boat and brought 1 officer and 1 P.O.* from the American destroyer.

Flying was cancelled for the day owing to weather conditions.

I put my name down for cricket, whether I will get a game or not I don't know?.

Kept the afternoon in the wheelhouse but did not take the wheel. I am cook today.

I also have the middle tonight, roll on Kure!!!

*Notes: Piped - the Boatswains call (or whistle) is a naval instruments used for ceremony and for sound signalling orders and commands throughout the ship.*
*Loaf - naval slang for hanging around aimlessly.*
*\*P.O. = Petty Officer*

### Tuesday 3rd August 1954

I had a change of jobs today, being put For'cl Heads and Bathroom sweeper. I worked very hard this forenoon.

I got my head down at 1300 until 1600 as I kept the middle watch.

I didn't feel too good when I mustered for the first dog.

Our aircraft have been machine gunning a splash target all day. Completing at 1730, after which we secured our splash target.

I closed up messdecks then went to the pictures on the flight deck.

The weather has been grim today, very clammy.

### Wednesday 4th August 1954

Up at 0400, did I feel chocker. Was lookout from 0600-0700 then the watch secured for breakfast.

Closed up for sleeve firings at 0800 which lasted until 1100, it was a competition shoot, I won nothing even though I hit the target? We were assessed on the whole.

I did no work this afternoon, as I was put in charge? I sunbathed on the upper deck and watched our Firefly fire rockets at the splash target. We have been right near the Korean coast all day.

I kept the last dog.

### Thursday 5th August 1954

Closed up for the forenoon watch and was lookout from 0800-0900 during which time both squadrons flew off, an air display was given by "Furies".

The watch on deck recovered the splash target wire. We entered the inland sea at approx 1200.

There was plenty of sport taking place on the flight deck this evening. I stayed on deck a couple of hours watching it.

Mustered for the first watch and was detailed as sea boats crew.

The weather has been very warm today.

## Friday 6th August 1954

Both watches fell in at 0715 for entering harbour, ship arrived alongside at 0830.

Provisions were brought onboard on arrival. A make and mend was given to the ship's company but I turned to as I was duty.

I was painting the ship's side in very warm weather, I have never felt so chocker in all my life.

The weather has been pretty grim today (too warm) roll on U.K.

## Saturday 7th August 1954

Captain's messdeck rounds at 1030.

Got my head down this afternoon.

Evans fetched me a music box and set of pearls for Barbara as I am still under stoppage.

After doing the last muster which was at 2100 I broke ship for "Flossie" Ford we had a wonderful run. We met Evans, Tolley and Scarth in Betty's Bar. I borrowed £1/1000yen from "Flossie".

Stayed ashore all night.

LESLIE EDWARD SMITH

# JAPAN BACK TO SINGAPORE

*"I must go down to the seas again, to the vagrant gypsy life,
To the gull's way and the whale's way where
the wind's like a whetted knife"*

*(John Masefield)*

◆ ◆ ◆

### Sunday 8th August 1954

Returned to the ship at 0645 and not a word was said.

Divisions were held in No 10s and was the sun hot.

We left Kure harbour at 1100 on our way to Singapore. I was working until 1200.

Got my head down this afternoon.

I kept the last dog, and was lookout from 1800-1900, the weather was very cool this evening. The ship left the inland sea at approx 1830.

### Monday 9th August 1954

Kept the forenoon watch in the wheelhouse, doing a **trick** of 1 and a half hours on the wheel.

Both our squadrons were flown off at 1330 for exercises against the ship.

Bofors aimers closed up for tracking exercise on our own aircraft, using the blind procedure.

One aircraft crashed into the barrier whilst landing on, there were no casualties.

There was plenty of sport played onboard this evening, deck hockey, volley ball, etc.

I kept the first watch and was lookout from 2200-2300. I wrote to Barbara.

**Note:** *A 'trick' is the naval name for a spell of duty, a watch, particularly as coxswain at the steering wheel.*

## Tuesday 10th August 1954

The amount of work I did this morning was NIL. Although the weather was very warm.

I kept the afternoon watch and have the middle tonight.

There was plenty of sport onboard this evening, I watched the squadron officers play each other 8" beat 825 3-1.

I went to the pictures on the flight deck to see the "Crimson Pirate" it was very good.

There was no flying today as our helicopter is not working.

## Wednesday 11 August 1954

I had a good middle last night, I slept most of the time.

I worked pretty hard in the **heads** this forenoon.

I am cook, how I hate the job!!

Kept my make and mend sleeping on the F.X. but it was very hot.

I had the first dog but did nothing special.

Cleared up messdecks for rounds.

I finished my punishment today, and I certainly am not sorry.

Went to the pictures on flight deck. The ship crossed Northern Formosa at 1200, the last we will see of land for a few days.

*Note:* Heads - naval name for latrines - originally sited in the extreme bow - or head - of the ship. The rating responsible for their general cleanliness is the Captain of the Heads.

## Thursday 12th August 1954

Up at 0400 and was lookout from 0500-0600. The watch on deck streamed the splash target.

We met HMS "Cockade" at approx 0730.

Both our squadrons were flown off at 0800 firing rockets etc at splash target. Mail was transferred to "Cockade" at 1200 she is taking it to Hong Kong for us.

Pay day today, I did not draw mine as I had no overalls in which to get paid.*

I kept the last dog after which I went to the pictures.

*There were strict dress codes for military Pay Parades.

## Friday 13th August 1954

The weather is wonderful this morning being much cooler than yesterday. I had the forenoon watch but did nothing special.

I went as minimuster for my pay at 1400 and drew £5, I owed 30/- and paid £2=7=0 for **slops**. I aren't going to get much of a run in Singapore.

I have the first watch, sea boats crew!

***Note:*** *Slops - naval name for any article of clothing (ready-made) which can be purchased from the ship's clothing store.*

### Saturday 14th August 1954

There was no messdeck rounds today but the 1st Lieut. walked round.

The ship's company changed their B.A.F.U.s to Malayan dollars today.

I had the afternoon and slept all the time.

The sea is very choppy today, and the ship has a steady roll on.

There was no sport played onboard this evening owing to the state of the weather.

### Sunday 15th August 1954

The hands secured at 0900. There was no divisions.

I slept during the afternoon, I kept the middle last night. At 1400 we had a very hard shower.

I had the first dog, sea boats crew.

Cleared up messdecks and flats at 2000 then I went to the cinema, the film "Top Secret".

The ship is expected in Singapore at 1100 tomorrow.

### Monday 16th August 1954

Up at 0400 and was detailed as the sea boats crew.

Both squadrons were flown off and will be landing ashore at Singapore. The ship entered harbour at 1300 and secured forward off the K.G.II dock. The weather was given.

On arrival in Singapore our crashed aircraft were disembarked.

I was employed till 1800 getting fresh veg onboard. I received 2 letters from Barbara and one from Mom.

Went to "Terror" canteen with Seager and got nice and drunk?

## Tuesday 17th August 1954

Felt rather groggy after my session last night but soon got over it.

I was employed in preparing the main seamen's mess for painting.

There was plenty of stores brought onboard today.

The seamen moved into the squadron mess whilst our mess is being sprayed.

I had a quiet evening onboard.

## Wednesday 18th August 1954

I was employed storing ship with Canteen stores.

It rained very hard first thing this morning.

The temperature began to rise at 1100, it was grim.

We started painting our mast today.

I am duty part of the watch, 1st Duty hand.

The duty hands had to get the seimmer (?) inboard as it was sinking.

Some of the duty post was detailed to secure the submarine "Taciturn" which came into harbour at 2100.

### Thursday 19th August 1954

I worked in the seamen's mess painting etc.

One half of the ship's company were employed storing ship.

I played hockey for the FX division and had a very good game seeing it was my first. We lost 2-0. The weather was terribly hot.

I went to "Terror" canteen at 1930 with "Brum" Davis and "Jan" Ropps, we had a couple of drinks then went to the pictures. I enjoyed it very much.

Searth lent me $5

### Friday 20th August 1954

I had an Xray **R.N.H.**

This forenoon I cleaned the P.O.s heads and bathrooms, and this afternoon I worked in the seamen's mess painting, it was very hot.

"I am cook of the mess". We have ammunitioned ship with **Hedge-Hogs** which will be dropped from our aircraft.

I slung a clean hammock this evening. I am really going to enjoy my night's sleep tonight.

*Notes:* R.N.H. - Possibly reference to 'Royal Naval Hospital' in Singapore.

*Hedgehogs - also known as Anti-Submarine Projector - was an anti-submarine weapon developed by the Royal Navy during world War II.*

### Saturday 21st August 1954

The hands were employed this forenoon in storing ship.

I worked in the P.O.s heads and bathroom until 1000 then I turned to in the main seamen's messdeck.

I got my head down on the castle deck this afternoon but didn't sleep very well as it was very warm.

I went to "Terror" canteen at 1930 with the lads and had a few pints, which I enjoyed very much.

Football commenced in UK today, I wish I were home now to watch some games.

### Sunday 22nd August 1954

The hands turned to for 1 hour securing at 0900.

I spent a very quiet forenoon doing nothing.

I slept like a log this afternoon. I received a letter from Barbara and was quite pleased.

I am duty Port today so I can go ashore.

### Monday 23rd August 1954

The ship's company started to paint ship, I was working on low lots and really enjoyed myself.

There was music being played to us from loud speakers on the jetty.

The sun was very hot all day and I got rather burned.

It rained very hard at 1600.

I borrowed $2 off Evans and went to "Terror" for a couple of drinks which went down very well indeed.

The "Warrior" put on a concert in Terror cinema, it went very well.

### Tuesday 24th August 1954

All the hands were over the side again today. The side at 1600 was two thirds finished.

The duty watch which was me were employed for one hour during the first dog.

I was carrying stages (?) inboard.

Borrowed $3 from Tolley and went into Singapore (Britannia Club) and got really blotto.

I arrived back onboard at 1130 and I had certainly had my fill!!!

## Wednesday 25th August 1954

I was very late in getting up this morning and wasn't feeling too good after my run ashore last night.

I was employed painting the latamaisons (?), and returning goods etc. The ship's side is almost finished with only a few minor details to be attended to.

I felt really tired tonight so I wrote a letter to Barbara after which I turned in.

*HMS Warrior - Painting the ship's side*

## Thursday 26th August 1954

Today the ship's side was completed.

The hands went to general payment at 1130 at which time an A.B. had a warrant and was awarded 10 days cells.

I drew £5, we were paid in B.A.F.U.S.

The commander told us how pleased he was. The effort made on painting ship was very good. I am duty tonight but have no special job.

The duty post were employed in moving paint during the 1st dog.

## Friday 27th August 1954

It has been a very quiet day with rain showers at frequent intervals.

There is a strong "buzz" going around that the ship is going to Indo China.

The Commander told the ship's company that our sailing for Hong Kong which was to be Monday 30th is now cancelled?

A make and mend was given onboard "Warrior" and I had a smashing afternoon rest.

I am staying onboard tonight to write to Barbara.

## Saturday 28th August 1954

There was no Captain's messdeck round today.

The Commander informed the ship's company that we are to proceed to Indo China to transfer refugees from Haiphong to Saigon.

The duty watch have worked until 1800 in preparation for our journey.

I went to "Terror" canteen with the lads and got really drunk.

When I got back onboard there was a letter from Barbara with some photos enclosed.

I wrote to Barbara tonight and told her how chocker I really were.

## Sunday 29th August 1954

Divisions today, dress 6s. C.inC. for East came onboard for the inspection (ADMIRAL LAMBE). He told us what our job would consist of regarding the transfer of the refugees.

Hands have been turned to all day helping to assemble temporary lavatories etc.

The weather has been very warm today, and quite a few chaps

fainted at divisions.

I saw a film show on the flight deck this evening, it was called "Botany Bay". All our air personnel left the ship and are staying in Singapore for our next trips.

### Monday 30th August 1954

I have worked with our explosive parties all day sending rockets ashore for our squadrons. The ship is almost ready for her trooping episode.

It has rained nearly all day, it cooled the ship down very much.

We had some 6000 blankets brought onboard, also 1500 camp beds. The blankets were returned because they were dirty (lousey).

There was also sanitary towels brought onboard in preparation for Indo China.

I am duty port tonight (Emergency Posts).

### Tuesday 31st August 1954

Beer was brought onboard this forenoon.

Wires were singled up at 1030.

We left Singapore at 1300, it was very warm.

Our squadrons flew overhead giving "Warrior" a send off.

I helped to stow beer all afternoon.

I had the first dog but had no special job to do.

After clearing up messdeck and flats, I went to the cinema.

LESLIE EDWARD SMITH

### Monday 30th AUGUST 1954

I have worked with an explosive parties all day. Loading rockets ashore for our squadron. The ship is almost ready for her Trooping episode.
It has rained nearly all day, it cooled the ship down very much.
We had some 6000 blankets brought onboard, also 1,500 camp beds. The blankets were returned because they were dirty (louses).
There was also Sanitary Towels brought onboard in preparation for Indo China.
I am duty port tonight. (Emergency Party).

### Tuesday 31st AUGUST 1954

Food was brought onboard this forenoon.
Divs were singled up at 1030.
We left Singapore at 1300, it was very warm.
The squadron flew over head giving "Warrior" a send off.
I have been to stow beds all afternoon. I had the first dog but had no special job to do.
After cleaning up mess deck & flats I went to the cinema.

DIARY OF AN ABLE SEAMAN - 1954

# SINGAPORE TO HAIPHONG

*"Our watch is on the ships that bear
the tools to beat the beast,
Our faith is in the men who make our trust an easy care,
Proclaim the need, the answer comes...............
Our Navy will be there."*

(Anonymous, Birmingham Mail, by "Bee")

◆ ◆ ◆

### Wednesday 1st September 1954

I was up at 0400, and did not get a lookout?

The ship is still being prepared for the embarkation of refugees.

I worked pretty hard this morning in preparation for Captain's rounds on Friday. I sunbathed nearly all afternoon.

I have the last dog in the wheelhouse and did one hour on the wheel.

A recording of the ship's concert was made this evening.

### Thursday 2nd September 1954

The weather was pretty rough this morning. I had the forenoon, and was employed in securing gear on the upper deck etc.

Saluting guns crews were closed up for drill at 0900.

I did not do much work today.

A bottle of beer was issued to the ship's company at 1800.

I found out that I am included in the refugee parties and have to be vaccinated.

We have also been detailed for cruising watches.

I was O.O.W. Messenger during the first and was I tired.

## Friday 3rd September 1954

Saturday routine was worked today, Captain's messdeck rounds.

I was vaccinated against small-pox, in the Hangar.

The ship's company had a make and mend but I had the afternoon watch and was turned to all afternoon.

At 1600 the Captain inspected the refugee quarters.

There are two cinema shows onboard tonight but I didn't go as I have the middle.

Gun Crews were closed up to repel aircraft at 0800. 2 Union Jacks were painted on our flight decks.

## Saturday 4th September 1954

The ship anchored at 0830 just off "Haiphong".

We met a French carrier on her way with refugees.

I was make and mend but did not get one owning to the embarkation of refugees.

A L.C.T. came alongside at 1300 with 900 onboard and at 1320 a L.C.T. with 600 onboard came port side to. I was employed helping people and their luggage up the gangway. It was a sight for sore eyes to see these people come onboard.*

We weighed and proceeded at 1700 and hit some roughers. BAD WEATHER.

I cleared up messdeck and turned in by 2030 was I tired.

*Note:* There are Pathe News and YouTube clips showing the refugees boarding. I couldn't see my father on any of the clips, and watching the footage made his diary entries even more real knowing he was there helping them on with their luggage.

*HMS Warrior and Landing Craft*

*Taking Vietnamese Refugees onboard*

## Sunday 5th September 1954

Up at 0400 this morning and was lookout from 0600-0700. It was a lovely morning. I went on the flight deck at 0900 to see the refugees being fed, and they certainly needed feeding.

Oriental music was played for them on the flight deck. Also the ship's band did some entertaining for a short period.

I slung my hammock on the FX this afternoon and had a wonderful sleep. Beer was issued at 1700. I kept the last dog and did lookout from 1900-2000 at 1930 we met two American ships carrying refugees.

LESLIE EDWARD SMITH

*Feeding time*

*Wash time*

DIARY OF AN ABLE SEAMAN - 1954

## Monday 6th September 1954

The weather is very fair and warm today.

I had the forenoon watch but no special job. Closed up for saluting gun drill at 1115.

The **"Buffer"** gave me a make and mend this afternoon because I turned to on Saturday.

I did some sun bathing on the flight deck.

The refugees were entertained this evening on the flight deck. A film cartoon was also put on for them. The lads gave the refugees toys etc.

*Note: Buffer - Naval nickname for the Cheif Bo'sun's Mate.*

---

Tuesday 7th SEPTEMBER 1954

The refugees were fed early this morning. A baby girl was born at 0240 weighing 6 lb. Mother and child were doing well. Ship stopped anchor at 0800. Refugees were disembarked by 0900. They were given cigs, Nutty and biscuits as a presents from "Warrior". Two French helicopters landed onboard at 0870. Bringing onboard the Naval liasion officer of Saigon. Mail was brought onboard at 1700. The ship was secured fore and aft and got under way at 1815.

## Tuesday 7th September 1954

The refugees were fed early this morning.

A baby girl was born at 0240 weight 6lb mother and child were doing well.

Ship dropped anchor at 0800. Refugees were disembarked by 1300 - they were given cigs, Nutty and biscuits as a present from "Warrior". Two French helicopters landed onboard at 0830 bringing onboard the Naval liaison officer of Saigon. Mail was brought on board at 1700.

The ship was secured for sea and got underway at 1815.

*Unusual battle honours for HMS Warrior!*

**Note:** *My father used to have a photo of the baby girl born onboard - the baby was framed by HMS Warrior life buoy, but sadly the photo has been mislaid.*

### Wednesday 8th September 1954

Warrior commissioned 1 year ago today. A special menu was served to the ship's company of Pork etc.

We took onboard 8000 tons of fuel oil from "Wave Knight" at 0900 finishing at approx 1300. We gave "Wave Knight" some books and magazines as she hasn't had any mail for 6 months.

I had a make and mend for doing the middle.

Beer was issued during the 1st dog, I drunk my bottle abreast the sea boat as I was on watch. I have to clear up messdeck tonight, I also have the morning watch.

### Thursday 9th September 1954

I kept the morning watch but didn't do a trick.

Saturday routine was worked, messdeck rounds which were done by the Commander.

The hands went to general payment at 1130, I drew £5=10=0.

A make and mend was given so I slept in my hammock.

I had the last dog and was lookout from 1930 to 2000 after which I went to the pictures on the flight deck, the film was "Reluctant Heroes".

### Friday 10th September 1954

The ship arrived at Haiphong at 0800 and dropped anchor.

The French Admiral of Indo China Command visited the ship.

Some 2000 refugees were embarked between 1300 and 1530, and was they in a state. They were "lousy".

The hands went swimming over the side for half an hour at 1800.

Both watches were fell in at 1830 and the ship weighted and proceeded fro Saigon.

Beer was issued to the ship's company.

I kept the first watch.

*Delousing*

## Saturday 11th September 1954

I kept the afternoon watch and was O.O.W. messenger during the last half of the watch. I learnt how to take a beasling (?)

I had a bottle of beer during the dogs. Went to the cinema with "Scupper" I got chocker so went and turned in.

There were two births onboard today. There was also one girl of 4 who died at 1145 and was buried at sea. It was said she died from pneumonia !!!

A Roman Catholic priest was in attendance at the burial.

## Sunday 12th September 1954

At 0620 this morning a girl of 5 months was buried at sea, she was also said to have died of pneumonia.

I wrote a letter to Mom.

I slept this afternoon on the F.X., was I tired after keeping the middle watch.

I was late mustering for the first dog. 1st dog watchman were employed in the hangar keeping the refugees in order for their evening meal.

I closed up messdecks for rounds, and have the morning watch.

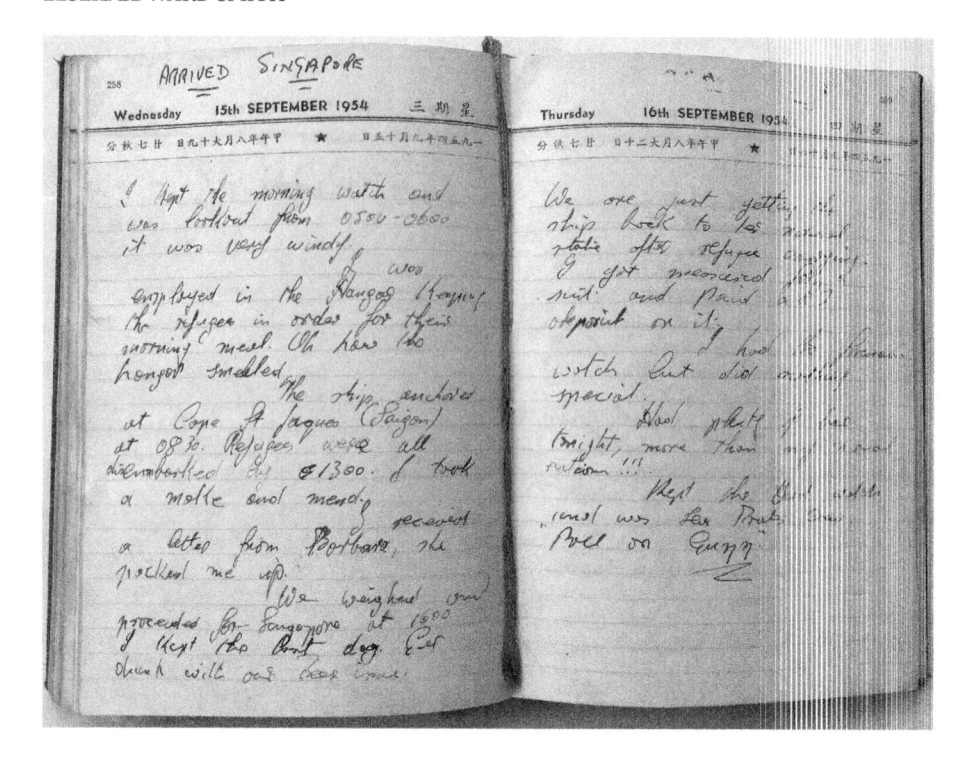

## ARRIVED SINGAPORE

### Wednesday 15th September 1954

I kept the morning watch and was lookout from 0500-0600, it was very windy.

I was employed in the hangar keeping the refugees in order for the morning meal. Oh how the hangar smelled.

The ship anchored at Cape St Jacques (Saigon) at 08430. Refugees were all disembarked by 1300. I took a make and mend.

I received a letter from Barbara, she packed me up.

We weighed and proceeded for Singapore at 1600. I kept the last dog. Got drunk with our Beer.

DIARY OF AN ABLE SEAMAN - 1954

*Feeding time.*

*"Oh how the hangar smelled".*

## Thursday 16th September 1954

We are just getting the ship back to her normal state after refugee carrying. I got measured for a suit and paid a £2 deposit on it.

I had the forenoon watch but did nothing special.

Had plenty of beer tonight more than my normal ration!!!

Kept the first watch and was Gun Boats Crew "Roll on Gunn".

## Friday 17th September 1954

Anti-Submarine devices (Refugees Heads) were taken ashore.

Flight deck was painted with non skid.

Two new barriers were brought onboard. I flung a clean hammock, or at least Tolley did?

Went to the pictures with the lads, it was grim.

### Saturday 18th September 1954

I got detailed to work in A.M.D.* and was finished by 0930.

The hands went to quarters clean gun at 1030 on completion a rehearsal for divisions was carried out on the flight deck.

I slept on the F.X. until 1530 after which I played Hockey for the FX division. We played the Stokers and lost 1-0. It was a very enjoyable game.

Went to the pictures to see "Band Wagon".

*A.M.D - possibly Air Mobility Division.

### Sunday 19th September 1954

The hands secured at 0900 and went divisions in No.6's. HMS Birmingham fired a 13 gun salute for the First Lord of the Admirals Mr J.L.P. Thomas, who came onboard Warrior for divisions.

I slept this afternoon on the cable deck, got up at 1630.

I am cook today and duty watch. I got a sub for duty watch and went to the canteen with the lads, we got rather drunk.

### Monday 20th September 1954

The "Birmingham" left for Hong Kong at 0830.

All our spare beer was taken ashore, which we had in Indo China.

Today has been very dull onboard with nothing exciting happening.

I started to paint the ship bathroom.

Went to the pictures with the lads on the flight deck this evening.

### Tuesday 21st September 1954

It rained very hard this morning for half an hour.

I have been employed painting the bathroom all day.

Lower deck was cleared at 1100, the hands mustered with camp beds as there have been 90 beds stolen.

I am duty tonight doing a sub for "Cooksley" but I have no special job.

Wrote to Barbara, this will most probably be my last letter to her?

### Wednesday 22nd September 1954

I have been employed in painting the chief's bathroom all forenoon.

The hands only worked until 1410 after which secured went. I slept till 1600 on the F.X.

Our squadron personnel joined the ship from "Simbang" Air Station.

Went to the cinema this evening.

# HAIPHONG TO HONG KONG

*"A life on the ocean wave,
A-home on the rolling deep!
Where the scater'd waters rave,
And the winds their revels keep."*

(Traditional Sea Shanty)

◆ ◆ ◆

## Thursday 23rd September 1954

We slipped and proceeded for Hong Kong at 0830.

It rained very hard so the hands did not fall in for leaving harbour.

Our squadrons flew onboard after we were clear of Singapore Roads.

The sea was choppy after leaving harbour.

I was employed getting up rockets from the magazines. It was a warm job!

We passed the Tanker that we saw being built in Kure during our stay there, she has a displacement of 32,000 tons.

### Friday 24th September 1954

I had a very good middle last night (sea boats crew).

I continued to paint out the Chief's bathroom this forenoon.

We commenced flying at 1300, the reason we did no flying this morning was because of bad weather.

I had a make and mend this afternoon and slept like a log.

During the first dog I was on the wheel, all our aircraft had flown onboard by 1615.

The ship's company were paid on the flight deck at 1700.

### Saturday 25th September 1954

Normal Saturday routine, negative rounds was worked.

I kept the morning and was lookout from 0500-0600.

Flying was commenced at 1300.

I slept all afternoon on the F.X.

The Captain addressed the ship's company on the flight deck. He told us we were to go home via South Africa, everyone onboard was very thrilled.

I had the last dog but no special job. Went to the cinema afterwards.

### Sunday 26th September 1954

Leave went at 0900. I have the forenoon on deck.

Both squadrons were flown off to Rocket practice. Our exhibition was given by Lt. Cdr. Wallace-Thompson, firing 16 rockets from his "Firefly".

Flying was completed by 1400.

I have the first watch and was lookout from 2000-2100. I got a blast from the O.O.W. for not doing my job properly.

I wrote a letter to Bill.

## Monday 27th September 1954

Flying was continued. One Firefly crashed into the barrier, there were no casualties.

I kept the afternoon watch.

Went to the cinema tonight with "Brum" Davies the film was the Gilbert and Sullivan Story.

I have the middle watch, roll on U.K.

## Tuesday 28th September 1954

I feel rather tired after my middle which I kept in the wheelhouse.

We flew off our squadron of Furies to intercept a force of R.A.F. planes which were attacking us from Hong Kong. At 0800 Gun Crews were closed up to repel aircraft.

The ship entered Hong Kong at 1500, it was very cool weather.

I went ashore with the lads and bought a civvy shirt and bow tie. I went to a dance it was very nice.

I was back onboard by 2400.

## Wednesday 29th September 1954

Ammunition was embarked today.

There seem to be quite a few people in cells after our first night in Hong Kong.

The amount of work I have done today is NIL. In fact I got my head down at 1400 and slept till 1600.

There has been plenty of traders onboard.

This evening was dull with really nothing to do.

### Thursday 30th September 1954

There hasn't been much to do, except to prepare for messdeck rounds which is taking place tomorrow.

There was no mail brought onboard today.

I took my watch to be repaired, it is going to cost me 12/6d.

Went to the cinema with the lads this evening, the film was "Executive Suite", it was very good.

### Friday 1st October 1954

Captain's messdeck rounds today, all went well.

A make and mend was given to the Starboard watch. I had a make and mend as I am now **Keyboard Sentry** until Tuesday.

I have the dogs, middle and forenoon, on the Keyboard and it is rather a tiring job.

The weather has been very cool all day, and it rained all evening.

There was quite a big fire in Kowloon. It was under control about 2400.

*Note: Keyboard Sentry - I believe this is a reference to special sentry duties carried out onboard ships - over the admiral's and captain's cabins, over the magazine keyboard and so on. They usually form the complete gun crew of one of the big turrets, and also man certain of the secondary armament and anti-aircraft guns.*

LESLIE EDWARD SMITH

# HONG KONG TO SINGAPORE

*"carry me over the seas, me boys,*
*To me true love far away,*
*For I'm takin' a trip on a Government ship*
*Ten thousand miles away."*

(Traditional Sea Shanty)

◆ ◆ ◆

### Saturday 2nd October 1954

The ship proceeded to be in company with HMS "Birmingham" and four destroyers.

I have the forenoon on the Keyboard.

At 0900 our squadrons flew off to intercept Vampires and Hornets which are to attack us from shore base. Gun crews closed up to repel aircraft, break up shot was fired. We had some men of the 7th Hussars and Ghurka regiment onboard to watch the exercise.

I slept this afternoon, was I tired.

Today men onboard "Warrior" have been given permission to wear the UN (Korean) medal.

### Sunday 3rd October 1954

We commenced flying at 0900, a display was given with a Fury dropping 2 500lb bombs, and a "Firefly" 16 rockets. One Fury crashed both barriers, there were no casualties.

I kept the afternoon watch on the Keyboard.

The ship entered Hong Kong at 1600.

I have finished doing Keyboard sentry as our Marines have now rejoined the ship.

There was no mail for me today.

### Monday 4th October 1954

Turned to in my Heads today, I did some painting.

I borrowed $10 from Tolley and bought gold badges and a pair of underpants.

A make and mend was given to the Port watch, the cable deck was in great demand for sleeping billets.

Was going to the pictures, but the weather didn't look very promising so we scrubbed round it.

Tolley wants me to enter in this Diary that I filled it in today, but I won't bother !!!!! (?)

### Tuesday 5th October 1954

I am cook of the mess, how I hate the job.

I have done practically no work at all.

I had the dogs on the Keyboard, which secured me for duty watch.

The beating of the retreat was carried out this evening on the flight deck. There were visitors onboard.

I went to the pictures this evening with "Brum" Davies.

### Wednesday 6th October 1954

Today our last day in Hong Kong has been rather dull, no-one has any money.

I was given a make and mend for doing keyboard sentry last night.

I spent my last 7/6d on T vests so roll on tomorrow, let get some pay.

### Thursday 7th October 1954

The hands fell in at 0730 and got the ship ready for sea.

We slipped at 0830 and proceeded for Singapore. We had quite a send off as we left Hong Kong harbour - Mary Ah Choy (Side Party) gave us a farewell.

We launched 4 Fireflies at 1600 landing on again at 1730.

I had the last dog O.O.W. messenger. I went to the pictures afterwards.

*Mary Ah Choy Side Party*

## Friday 8th October 1954

Flying for today was cancelled. It has been very hot.

The ship's company got paid in Sterling today, I picked up £5=0=0 so I paid £2 on my owing suit. I also got my watch out of repair costing me 12/6d.

I kept the forenoon and first.

Clocks were put back half an hour at 1815.

## Saturday 9th October 1954

4 "Fireflys" were launched at 0900 landing on again at 1100.

I had afternoon watch.

Today I believe is Jean Froggat's wedding day.

There was plenty of sport on the flight deck this evening, deck hockey etc.

I went to the cinema to see "Blackbeard the Pirate" it was very good. I have the middle watch.

*Note: Jean Frogatt was the daughter of my father's older sister Lucy, and she was the sister of singer/songwriter Raymond Froggatt*

### Sunday 10th October 1954

The weather has been perfect today, and the sea flat calm.

I slept all afternoon because I had the middle last night.

I was in the wheelhouse for the first dog and did a 40 minute trick on the wheel.

Cleared up messdecks after which I went to the cinema.

### Monday 11th October 1954

I was up at 0400, sea boats crew.

Flying was commenced at 0800 Fireflys only were launched. They carried out exercises on the ship.

I got my issues of pyjamas today. Went for a dental inspection and was dentally fit.

I have the last dog tonight.

### Tuesday 12th October 1954

The ship anchored in Singapore Roads at approx 0730 and took onboard 30,000 galls of Avgas.

The ship went to a bury (?) on completion of fuelling being secured by 1600.

I went ashore with "Brum" Davies. We first went to Ne-soon and bought some **Rabbitts,** then we went into Singapore (Britannia

Club) and got rather drunk.

What a run we had.

I received a letter from Barbara, it will most probably be my last.

**Note:** Rabbits - naval slang given to articles taken ashore privately (contraband).

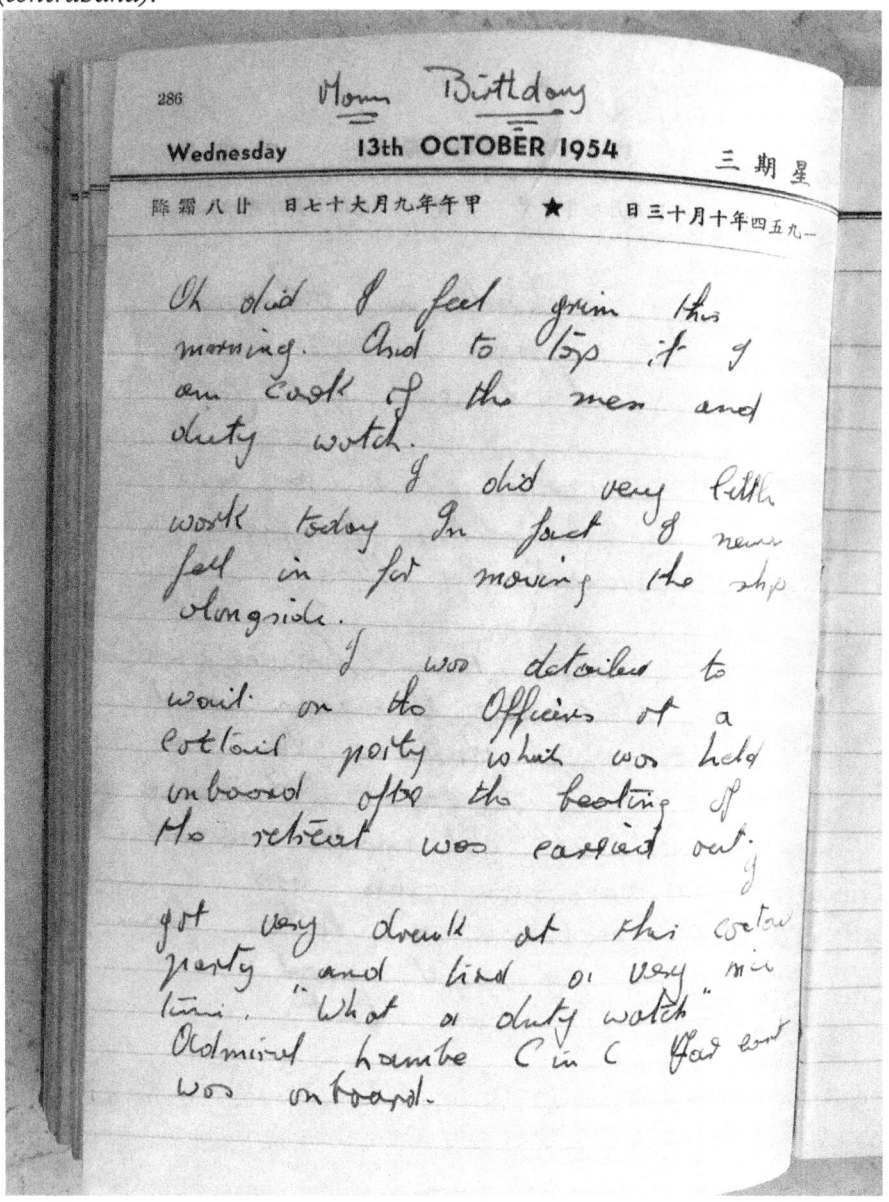

## Mom's Birthday

### Wednesday 13th October 1954

Oh did I feel grim this morning. And to top it I am cook of the mess and duty watch.

I did very little work today. In fact I never fell in for moving the ship alongside.

I was detailed to wait on the Officers at a cocktail party which was held onboard after the beating of the retreat was carried out.

I got very drunk at this cocktail party and had a very nice time. "What a duty watch".

Admiral Lambe C in C Far East was onboard.

*C in C's Far East Inspection*

### Thursday 14th October 1954

I feel pretty good after my small(?) session last night?

Most of the hands have been employed in storing ship today in preparation for our departure to South Africa.

I worked quite hard in the head for a change !!!

I bought two silver ships onboard with my last $5.

I went to a film onboard to see "Will Any Gentleman".

There was mail onboard at 2030.

### Friday 15th October 1954

There has been plenty of fresh provisions embarked ready for our trip to South Africa.

3 Furys were taken ashore (crashed).

The ship's side was touched up here and there to give us a bit smarter appearance.

I went to the pictures this evening onboard to see "An American in Paris", it was grim.

I slung a clean hammock.

DIARY OF AN ABLE SEAMAN - 1954

# SINGAPORE TO SOUTH AFRICA

### *(Durban - Port Elizabeth - Simonstown - Dakar)*

> *"Don't you call us common sailors anymore*
> *Good things to you we bring*
> *Don't you call us common men*
> *We're as good as anybody that's on shore"*
>
> *(Traditional Sea Shanty - Common Sailors)*

◆ ◆ ◆

### Saturday 16th October 1954

A few more provisions were brought onboard.

The ship got underway for South Africa at 1030. We had quite a send off.

I had the forenoon watch which was kept on the FX. Our watch secured the anchor for sea.

I played deck hockey this evening, we beat the boat party 1-0, it was a very nice game.

I was O.O.W. messenger during the first watch for 2 hours 2000-2200. There was quite a strong wind blowing as we proceeded up the Malacca Straits.

### Sunday 17th October 1954

It has been a very quiet day for me, secure went at 0900 and from then on I read a book called "Lady Chatterley's Lover"

I kept the afternoon watch in the wheelhouse and did a trick of 1 hour and ten minutes on the wheel.

4 Fireflys were launched late in the forenoon, landing on at approx 1330.

### Monday 18th October 1954

We had a rendezvous with HMS "Glory" at 0800 and transferred our mail to her. She is Singapore bound and is loaded with supplies.

Both squadrons were flown off at 1000.

I had a make and mend and slept on the FX.

Flying was completed by 1600 at which time "Warrior" altered course to port for South Africa. I kept the first dog on deck and was employed in rigging the .22 range on the flight deck.

.22 competition commenced today. One aircraft dropped depth charges, there were no fish?

### Tuesday 19th October 1954

I was up at 0400, morning watch, but had no special job.

The hands went to emergency stations and D.C.State (1) was assumed. The Commander gave a speech regarding the way in which abandon ship should be carried out.

The sea has been very choppy, we have quite a roll on. We are at present in the Bay of Bengal. I had the last dog, after which I went to see "The Great Caruso".

## Wednesday 20th October 1954

The sea is still very choppy so all flying has been cancelled for the day.

At 1205 "Warrior" passed over the line (Equator) into King Neptune Kingdom. King Neptune visit to "Warrior" has been delayed owing to our programme but he is coming onboard after we leave Cape Town.

I worked with the Bosun Party on the QDD all afternoon.

I have the first watch tonight.

## Thursday 21st October 1954

Gun functioning trials were carried out each mounting firing 8 rounds per barrel (on the horizon).

The ship's company were paid at 1130, I drew £5=0=0 and paid £2=0=0 on my suit. I also had a fitting for my suit.

I kept the afternoon watch and have the middle tonight.

I am cook of the mess today, it's a lousy job.

The sea is still rather choppy but it is to be expected as we are now in the Indian Ocean.

## Friday 22nd October 1954

Flying for the day was cancelled owing to weather conditions.

I had a make and mend as I kept the middle watch. I slept on the FX. During the first dog I worked rigging the .22 rifle range.

We have run into a couple of scrawly showers through the dog. "Warrior" is near the centre of the Indian Ocean.

I cleared up messdecks and flats for rounds.

## Saturday 23rd October 1954

Normal Saturday routine was worked negative messdeck rounds.

Flying programme was cancelled owing to swell.

I had the morning watch and was lookout from 0500 to 0600.

I slept during the afternoon on the FX.

It has been quite a day for sport onboard "Warrior" with all sorts of events being held on the flight deck.

I had the last dog after which I went to the cinema.

King Neptune came onboard today and the Captain was put on a charge for creating a disturbance in his Kingdom.

*Crossing the Equator, 1954*

*King Neptune*

DIARY OF AN ABLE SEAMAN - 1954

*Fun in the sun at the Equator*

LESLIE EDWARD SMITH

*Fancy dress fun - Crossing the Equator*

DIARY OF AN ABLE SEAMAN - 1954

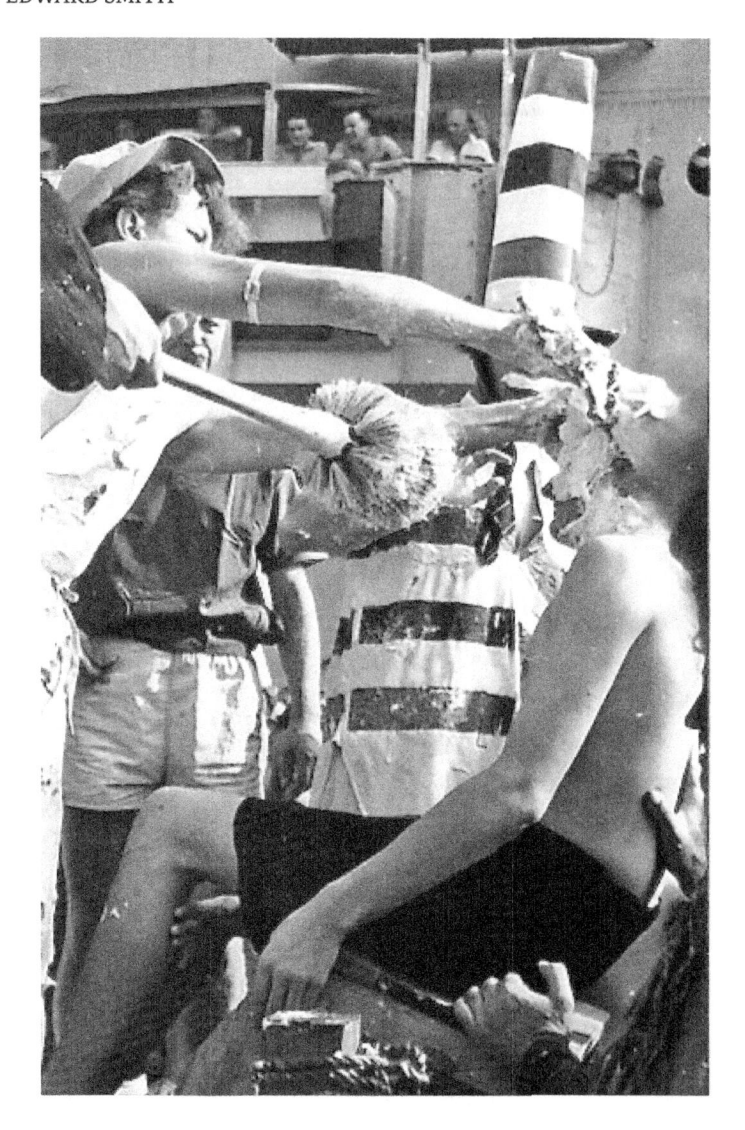

*Being roughly lathered and shaved, Crossing the Equator*

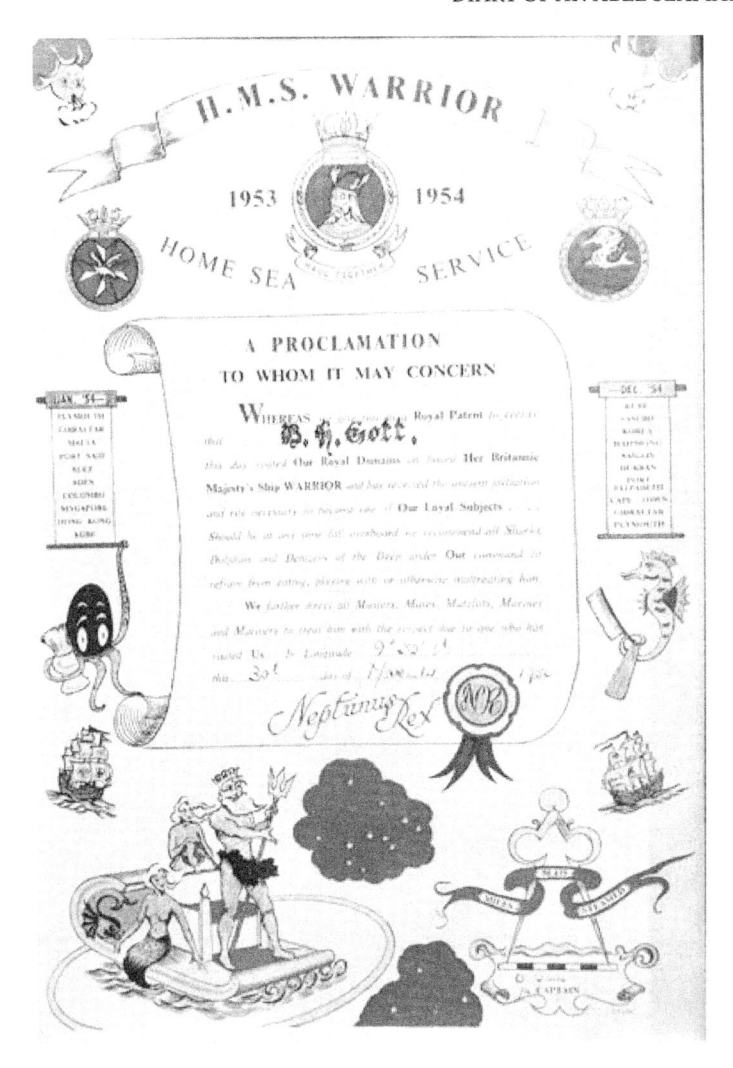

"Crossing the Line" certificate issued to B. H. Gott on November 30, 1954

## Sunday 24th October 1954

I had the forenoon watch which I kept in the wheelhouse. I did 2 hours on the wheel, she was rather difficult to keep on course.

Divisions were held onboard, dress No 10s after which the Captain addressed the ship's company.

I slept this afternoon, there was nothing else to do.

I had the first watch but no special job.

## Monday 25th October 1954

I scrubbed paintwork all forenoon in preparation for rounds on Wednesday.

I had the afternoon watch and have the middle to go with it.

Flying was cancelled for today as visibility was very bad, there was also quite a heavy swell.

Medical inspection of the ship's company commenced.

## Tuesday 26th October 1954

I got the Bathroom and Heads ready for the rounds tomorrow.

The hands went to flying stations at 1300 and both squadrons flew off. Our flying programme was carried out off the Northern tip of "Mauritius".

Flying was completed by 1600 and we continue our course for South Africa.

I had a make and mend. I also had the first dog but no special job.

I done a **PULHEEM** today and passed A.1.

**Note:** PULLHEEMS - a system for assessing mental and physical health, it is an acronym **P**hysique, **U**pper limbs, **L**ower limbs, **H**earing (right), **H**earing (left), **E**yesight right, **E**yesight left, **M**ental function, **S**tability (emotional).

## Wednesday 27th October 1954

I kept the morning watch (Sea Boats Crew).

Flying commenced at 0800 and finished at 1200. I had an unofficial make and mend!!

I had the last dog and was lookout from 1900-2000.

I went to the cinema this evening to see "David and Bathsheba".

### Thursday 28th October 1954

Saturday routine was worked, Captain did messdeck rounds.

The messdeck party were given a make and mend which was me.

Flying commenced at 0800 and was completed by 1000.

Nets have been rigged under all gun sponsors in preparation for painting tomorrow.

The ship is expecting to anchor off Madagascar for painting.

I have the first watch.

### Friday 29th October 1954

The ship was stopped in a heavy sea and the hands went over the side to paint.

We passed the Southern Coast of Madagascar at 0800.

Painting was completed by 1030 and the ship got underway again at 1100.

I had the afternoon watch and was employed in stowing away stages (?) etc.

I am cook of the mess.

A ship's "concert" was held in the hangar, I went and it was very good.

I have the middle watch tonight.

### Saturday 30th October 1954

I closed up for drill on the saluting guns at 0730.

Normal Saturday routine was worked, upper-deck rounds were carried out by the Captain.

I slept all afternoon on the FX.

I slept down the messdeck tonight as it was rather cold on the FX with quite a strong wind blowing.

## Monday 1st November 1954

The ship entered Durban harbour at 0800. The **Lady in White** sang us into harbour, it was very pleasant.

There have been people along to see the ship all day. This is the first time a ship has visited Durban since 1946.

I went ashore at 1700 with "Jon" Rapps and found Durban to be very dull and quiet. I returned onboard by 2400 feeling very tired.

***Note:*** *The Lady in White was Perla Siedle Gibson, a South African soprano and artist who became internationally celebrated during the Second World War as the Lady in White, when she sang troopships in and out of Durban harbour.*

## Tuesday 2nd November 1954

I got detailed for **Boot Topping** party, what a messy job it was.

A 7-Gun Salute was fired for the French Consul and an 11-Gun Salute was fired for O.C. S.A. Natal Forces (Naval).

A make and mend was given to the starboard watch and leave granted from 1315.

I am duty watch tonight and was detailed to ???? the jetty, it was an embarrassing job?

I am emergency Porty (?). A Cocktail Party was held onboard this evening.

**Note:** Boot Topping seems to have been a line painted on warships

## Wednesday 3rd November 1954

I went ashore with Evans and Dillon this evening and had a very nice time.

We had a little drinking session in the afternoon and came back onboard to change from No 10s to No 2s. I borrowed "Brum" Bannister's suit.

*Photo of my father with two ship-mates in Durban 1954 - so maybe this photo is the one with Evans and Dillon in? ... in their "No 2s" ? My father is on the left, winking.*

## Thursday 4th November 1954

The hands got paid today. I drew £5=0=0. A make and mend was given to the starboard watch. I was employed during the afternoon working over the side.

I went ashore at 1600 with Evans and Scarth, we went to an open air dance, it was most enjoyable.

I was very late in getting back onboard.

### Friday 5th November 1954

I had a make and mend this afternoon, and slept like a log.

The ship opened to visitors at 1400 and 3000 people came onboard.

I went ashore with all the lads at 1700 and did we get drunk.

November the 5th was celebrated here just as in UK, there were plenty of fireworks being let off ashore.

### Saturday 6th November 1954

The ship opened to visitors at 1400 and I was guide. We had 6000 people come onboard. The weather was absolutely first class.

I am duty Post and cook of the mess, roll on tomorrow, let's get ashore.

I am 2nd duty Hand.

### Sunday 7th November 1954

Normal Sunday routine, Negative divisions was worked.

I borrowed £1 off "Jon" Rapps and went ashore with Evans & Tolley at 1200. We went onto the beach and sunbathed all afternoon, it was a beautiful day.

We returned onboard at 1700 to find quite a queue of people trying to get onboard.

Evans, Tolley, Dillon and myself went ashore again at 1800 in No

3s. We went to the Durban Jockey Club and got very drunk there. We returned onboard ship at 2400.

## Monday 8th November 1954

We left Durban harbour at 0900 and what a wonderful send off we had. The Lady in White sang us out.

The weather was pretty rough on leaving harbour, all the hands were employed in securing the ship for sea.

I scrubbed paintwork in the messdeck during the afternoon.

I kept the last dog in the wheelhouse and did half hour on the wheel, she was rather difficult to keep on course.

Warrior had approx. 140000 visitors onboard during our stay in Durban.

## Tuesday 9th November 1954

The ship anchored off East London after a very rough night at sea. the Captain addressed the ship's company.

Anchor was weighed at 0930 and we proceeded to sea, squadrons were flown off to give exhibition over East London and Port Elizabeth. All aircraft landed on by 1230, there was one crash but no casualties.

The sea is very much calmer today.

I have the first watch.

## Wednesday 10th November 1954

The ship arrived in Port Elizabeth Harbour at 0800. There was quite an audience watching us come in. Four HAVARD Aircraft of the S.A.A.F. flew over "Warrior".

A salute of 7 guns was made to a Swedish official who came

onboard. Cricket and Rifle teams were loaded ashore this afternoon.

I took a make and mend !!!

I am duty watch tonight but have no special job.

This is the first time an aircraft carrier has ever visited Port Elizabeth.

## Thursday 11th November 1954

Leave was given to the Port watch from 1300 whilst the Starboard watch were turned to.

I went to the Ford Motor Works to watch the assembly of the cars, it was most interesting. We were given tea afterwards.

I borrowed £1 from "Jon" Rapps and stayed ashore with Evans & Rapps, we got very drunk and went to a Navy dance, there were plenty of girls there and we really enjoyed ourselves.

I got back onboard at 2400.

The ship has been opened to visitors, 11000 came onboard.

## Friday 12th November 1954

Leave was granted to the Starboard watch whilst the Port watch worked on the ship's side. I worked under the bows in nets, it was a grim job.

A children's party was held onboard for orphans etc. Some 2000 children came onboard and were given tea. Shows swings etc were rigged.

The beating of the retreat took place on the jetty at 1800 in front of an audience of 2000, everyone seemed very impressed.

I went ashore at 1900 with Evans, we went to the pictures to see

"The Belles of St Trinians".

### Saturday 13th November 1954

The ship left Port Elizabeth harbour at 0900, there was quite an audience on the jetty cheering us out. The ship's company gave 3 cheers to the citizens of P.E.

I closed up in the wheelhouse on leaving harbour and did half an hour on the wheel.

I slung my hammock on the FX this afternoon and slept like a log.

I had the first watch and was lookout for the first hour, it was very cold.

### Sunday 14th November 1954

The hands worked till 0930 today.

The ship has been off Cape Town since 1200.

I have got earache today and feel grim to top it all I am cook of the mess.

Our flying programme has been cancelled owing to bad weather.

I slung me a clean hammock.

### Monday 15th November 1954

The hands were called at 0530, was I tired, I kept the middle.

The ship entered harbour at 0645, there were very few people about. No 3s were worn for entering harbour.

I saw the doctor with my earache, he gave me special treatment.

I had a make and mend and slept in my hammock. Did I need it.

The ship opened to visitors at 1300, we had a steady flow

onboard until 1800.

I stayed onboard as I didn't feel much like a run ashore.

I saw the M.O. this morning with my ear and am still getting treatment.

I closed up at saluting guns at 1000 and an 11 gun salute was fired for the Mayor.

I took a make and mend this afternoon but could not sleep with my bad ear. I received treatment again at 1700.

The weather has been very warm with temperature reach the 80s.

The Mayor and Town Clerk came onboard by our helicopter.

## Wednesday 17th November 1954

A children's party was held onboard all went well.

I took a make and mend and slept like a log.

The hands were paid in the Hangar at 1130, I drew £6=0=0.

I paid £3 what I owed and £2 on my suit leaving me with £1, so I went ashore with the lads and had quite a run. I stayed ashore the night.

## Thursday 18th November 1954

I felt grim this morning as I have had no sleep.

I caught the train back to Cape Town at 0610 and arrived at 0645.

I went to Holy Mass* which was held onboard.

The ship was opened to visitors at 1300 and I was required to act as guide seeing that I am duty post. We had some 12000 people onboard in brilliant sunshine.

The beating of the retreat ceremony was carried out on the jetty in front of an audience of about 4000, it was a success.

*My father was raised a Catholic by his mother, and went to a Catholic School. All his life he held some affinity, but never practised or attended church after I was born. He had a Catholic funeral however, with a Requiem Mass.*

## Friday 19th November 1954

The ship left Cape Town at 1000 with some 150 S.A. officers and men of all the services for exercises "shop window". On leaving harbour 3 fireflys were launched by men of R.A.T.O.G. and catapult etc. Bombs were dropped, rockets fired. Also all Port Armament engaged our own aircraft with break-up shot. Our visitors were very impressed with our display.

The ship anchored in the Bay at Simonstown at 1600. I went ashore with Tolley and "Mick" Mills, we went to a dance which was most enjoyable.

A nice evening followed the Dance.

*HMS Warrior at Simonstown*

### Saturday 20th November 1954

I returned onboard at 0400 after having had a very nice time ashore.

There was no messdeck rounds.

It has been a very quiet day onboard with most of the lads ashore.

(Plymouth Argyle beat Birmingham 1-0)

### Sunday 21st November 1954

Normal Sunday routine was worked Negative divisions. Secure went at 0930.

I slept during the afternoon.

The ship opened to visitors at 1300, also side shows were put on for a few children. The ship closed to visitors at 1600.

I went ashore with the boys at 1830 and we all got pretty drunk although we had a very nice evening.

I returned onboard at 0030, it was raining slightly but very cold.

### Monday 22nd November 1954

The ship left Simonstown harbour at 1030 for Dakar which is going to take 11 days. On leaving harbour we ran into some rough weather, the ship has quite a good roll and pitch on.

I have the afternoon watch but no special job.

(I am Cook of the Mess). The ship altered course at 1300 for Dakar which helped to take some roll off, even though the roll mainly still remained.

Tombola was played this evening.

### Tuesday 23rd November 1954

Today has been rather dull. I had a make and mend this afternoon and slept in the mess.

I had the first dog but no special job.

The sun was shining very nicely this evening. The ship ran into a big shoal of dolphins at 1630.

It was stated in the Daily orders that the present journey from Simonstown to Dakar is 3695 miles.

### Wednesday 24th November 1954

I was up at 0400 morning watchman and was lookout from 0400-0500, it was pretty warm.

Today has been very quiet onboard with nothing special happening.

I kept the last dog.

### Thursday 25th November 1954

I did a "Kit" muster this forenoon, borrowing a couple of items to complete my Kit. All went well.

I went to the pictures at 1900 to see "Alice in Wonderland" (Cartoon).

During the first watch I was lookout for the 1st hour, the boat was not exercised during this watch.

AVGAS tanks were flooded with sea water to get rid of remaining AVGAS.

### Friday 26th November 1954

All morning I have been preparing my bathroom for rounds

tomorrow.

The P.O. of the messdeck party had the middle last night, so I had a make and mend !!!!

I went to the cinema this evening to see "Across the Wide Missouri"

More of our AVGAS tanks were floated during the course of the afternoon, they should all be complete by the time the ship arrives in Dakar.

## Saturday 27th November 1954

Saturday messdeck rounds were carried out by the Commander. The Captain is sick.

I had a make and mend and slept all afternoon.

The weather has been warm today as the ship is now nearing the equator.

I had the first dog but no special job.

I cleared up messdeck & flats.

AVGAS tank were washed out again today.

## Sunday 28th November 1954

I was up at 0400 morning watch. I stowed hammocks.

Divisions were held onboard, dress No 10s. The Commander took the Salute.

I slept on the FX in my hammock during the afternoon, it was very warm.

Everyone was sun bathing on the upper deck today.

I kept the last dog and have all night in.

### Monday 29th November 1954

I put in a request for a draft on to HMS St Austell Bay on arrival in UK.

The hands went to general payment on the flight deck at 1130. We were paid our Korean gratuity. I drew £15 and finished paying for my civvy suit, plus paid Tolley £2=0=0 which I owed him from Cape Town.

The ship crossed the equator at approx 2100.

The weather has been very warm, the temperature reached about 85 degrees.

I had the 1st watch.

### Tuesday 30th November 1954

The hands secured at 0840 and at 0900 King Neptune his Queen and followers came onboard. The remainder of the forenoon was one big skylark.

I was thrown into the bath at 1100 thus receiving my customary welcome from his Majesty.

I am cook of the mess.

Kept the afternoon watch but slept seeing as there was a general make and mend.

The was a sing song on the flight deck this evening. I went and enjoyed myself very much.

*...being "thrown in the bath"?*

## Wednesday 1st December 1954

I saw the Commander this morning about my request to commission "**St Austell Bay**", he is forwarding my name.

Quarter ......(clear?) Gun went out at 0900 and exercise fire in the magazines was carried out.

D.C. State (1) was exercised.

I had a make and mend as I kept the middle last night.

I won 10/- on England beating Germany 3-1.

I have a grim cold.

**Note:** *My father never did serve on St Austell Bay ship.*

## Thursday 2nd December 1954

Up at 0400 morning watchman. I had the last hour lookout.

The ship increased speed at 1400 to get as near as 60 miles from Dakar as we have a rating with an acute appendicitis.

I had last dog but no special job.

The helicopter took off at 1700 and landed at 1830 and is remaining ashore for the night.

The Commander addressed the ship's company on the flight deck.

### Friday 3rd December 1954

The helicopter landed on at 0700 there was a very strong wind blowing.

A 21 gun salute was fired to the French flag. A 21 gun salute was returned.

The ship got into harbour at 0900 and secured starboard side too.

I received 2 letters, one from Bill and 1 from Mom.

A cocktail party was held onboard this evening.

### Saturday 4th December 1954

There were no messdeck rounds today.

The ship opened to visitors at 1300 and I was duty as I was detailed as a guide. 1000 people visited the ship.

I went to a cinema show on the flight deck.

I lent "Brum" Seager £2.

### Sunday 5th December 1954

Normal Sunday routine was worked Negative divisions.

The hands secured at 0900.

The ship opened to visitors at 1300 and there were quite a few people onboard compared with yesterday.

I slept during the afternoon on the FX.

# SOUTH AFRICA TO UK

*"I must go down to the seas again, to the vagrant gypsy life,*
*To the gull's way and the whale's way where*
*the wind's like a whetted knife;*
*And all I ask is a merry yarn from a laughing fellow-rover,*
*And quiet sleep and a sweet dream when the long trick's over."*

(John Masefield)

♦ ♦ ♦

### Monday 6th December 1954

The ship left Dakar at 0920 and proceeded to UK.

The sea was choppy after we left the mainland.

Paybook of the 1st ......(?)* party were put into the MAA's office to have leave marked in.

I kept the last dog in the wheelhouse and did half hour on the wheel.

\* Photo of illegible word:

### Tuesday 7th December 1954

I made out my custom duty list.

Today has been very quiet with nothing out of the ordinary happening.

I kept the first watch and was employed in preparing the wardroom for paying.

The ship will reach the Canary Isles tomorrow evening.

### Wednesday 8th December 1954

D.C. State (1) was exercised by the Engine Room Dept.

I had afternoon watch but took an unofficial make and mend.

I am cook of the mess the last time before the ship arrives in "Guzzy".

The ship passed a mountain which was on our port side at 1600, this was the first in the Canary isles series and was some 12000 feet in height.

I have the middle watch.

### Thursday 9th December 1954

I was put light Duty this morning with a poison leg.

The ship hit roughers and rolled something grim with waves breaking over the flight deck.

The ship is about 150 miles from G.B.

### Friday 10th December 1954

Saturday messdeck rounds were exercised by the Captain.

The weather is still pretty rough. The ship at 0800 was just off Gibraltar.

A make and mend was given.

### Saturday 11th December 1954

Upper deck rounds were carried out by the Captain.

I came off light Duty.

At 1600 the ship entered the Bay of Biscay and the sea was fairly calm.

Birmingham beat Liverpool 9-1. I also won the Sweep which was £4=10=0.

I went to the cinema show onboard this evening the film was "Scrooge".

### Sunday 12th December 1954

No divisions were held onboard, the hands secured at 0900. I did not turn to?

The ship left the Bay 1200 and entered the English Channel at 1600, the sea was choppy with a cold wind blowing onto our Port side, we passed many ships through the past 24 hours.

We are expecting to arrive at Portsmouth at 0800 in the morning.

### Monday 13th December 1954

Both squadrons were flown off at 0800, the ship being some 30 miles off Portsmouth.

On completion of flying the ship entered Portsmouth harbour and anchored at 1100. The Customs came onboard to deal with squadron personnel.

The Captain addressed the ship's company. I took a make and mend. The hands were employed painting ship's side in pouring rain.

We left Portsmouth at 1800 for Plymouth E.T.A 0800 tomorrow.

**NOTE: The 13th December was the final entry in my father's diary.**

.....however the very final entry in the Diary is one on the very last page under "NOTES" - I did a drawing on 16th October 1965, aged six years old, in wax crayons of a ship:

DIARY OF AN ABLE SEAMAN - 1954

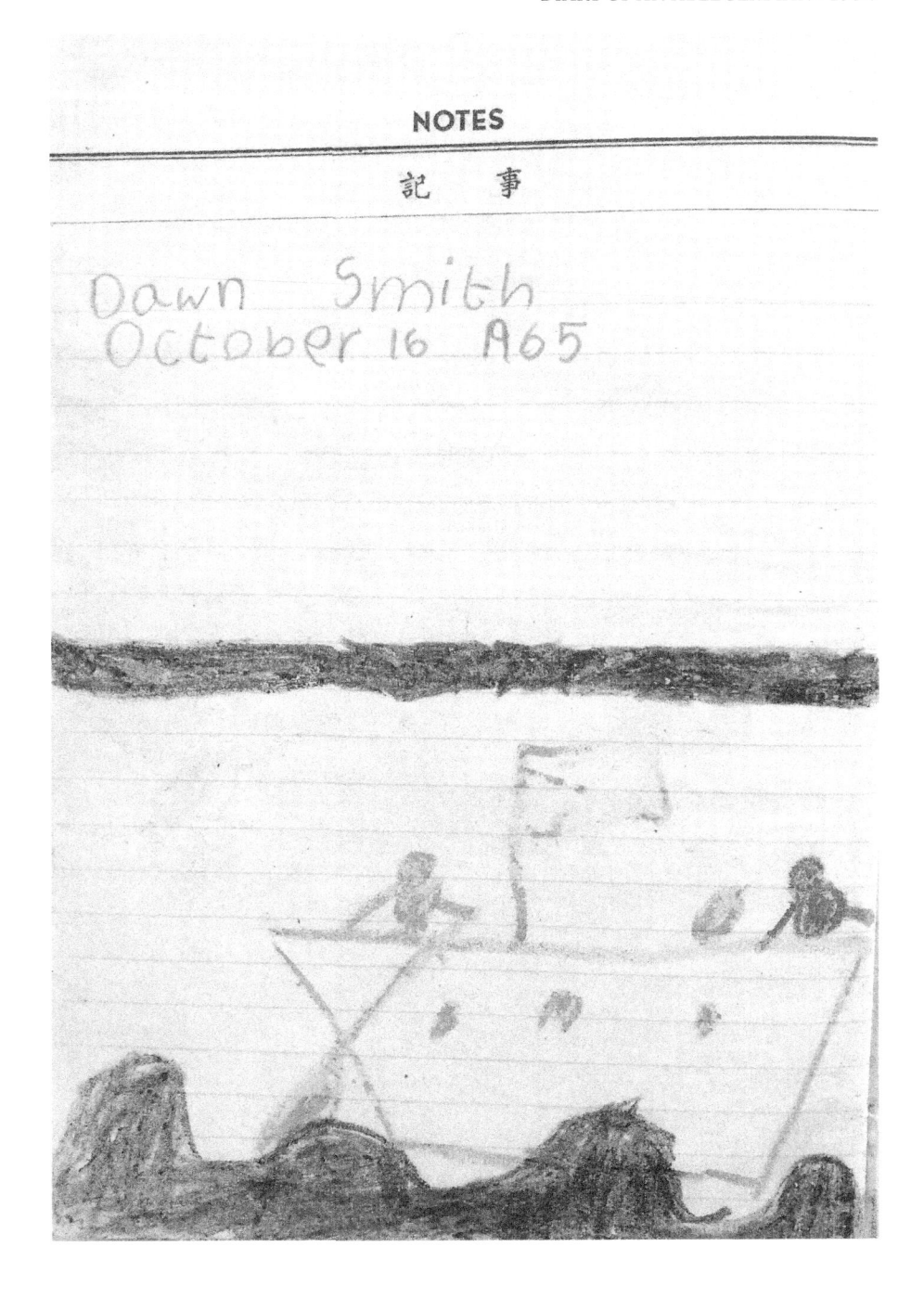

**NOTES**

記　事

Dawn Smith
October 16 A65

# AFTERWORD

Having typed out my father's diary, certain aspects made an impact on me and challenged me to think a bit deeper about my parents.

We read in the diary that my mother ended her engagement with Les (I was never nearly born!). However, they obviously got back together and married a year later in 1955. I was born in 1959, then a stillborn daughter (due to toxaemia) followed in 1962 (Diane), and then my sister, Elizabeth, was born in 1967.

My parents settled into a happy family life for many years and my sister and I had a very happy childhood. My father enjoyed family life and gardening. He built a greenhouse and grew tomatoes, and marrows, and also cultivated a vegetable patch with runner beans and other vegetables. He still enjoyed a drink and a smoke - but these were strictly reserved for weekends, and even then only very moderately: ten Goldleaf and a couple of pints of ale from the Outdoor up the road.

Like many of their generation, coming through WW2 left emotional scars - for my father, it was experiencing the sheer terror that he was going to die when the bombers came over during air raids. He told me - not long before he died - how in the Andersen shelter he would hear them approaching overhead, then the bombs would fall and he said he felt such anger against them that he held his fist up to the ceiling and swore at the bombers to go away. My mother was traumatised by being evacuated (my father wasn't evacuated). Along with her two sisters, she was sent to Wales and they weren't very happy away from home. She remembers waving goodbye to her mother on the train platform in Birmingham, and all three sisters travelled together, very fearful - not knowing when they would see their parents again.

The diary is a mixture of recording life onboard ship plus life ashore - including drinking escapades in between jobs on the ship. However, I do not judge my father for his over-indulgence in alcohol and his frequent hangover as it was the culture of the day for many back then.

I was struck by how my father - a healthy 23-year-old fattened up on good naval food - often records feeling very tired. I wondered if this was particularly due to the watches he was required to keep at 4 am. These watches during the night can affect a person's circadian rhythm so I put a lot of the tiredness onboard down to that…….and of course, his late-night excessive drinking bouts didn't help with fatigue!

Another thing I noted is that I never knew my father to go to church at all - he was brought up as a Catholic and attended a Catholic school and was taught by Nuns. He always said "I'm a Catholic I am" but he never went to a single Mass once he was married. However, in the diary, he records going to "Holy Mass" so his faith obviously meant something to him at that time.

I sense that after my mother ends her engagement the mood in the diary changes somewhat. Les records nothing about how this affected him, but it obviously went deep and I picked up reading between the lines that he was keen to get back home and sort things out.

My father records a series of minor misfortunes throughout the diary, but in such a deadpan way that it can read as quite comical at times: from being bitten by mosquitoes, getting battered legs from a game of hockey, enduring punishments for his often misdemeanours (at one point humping scram bag gear all day) or being 'cook of the mess' (a job he hated), he was frequently skint having to borrow money, plus a few minor ailments (earache, painful vaccinations, a "grim cold" and an eye problem) - all this contrasted with some highlights: a trip up Kandy (a beautiful part of Sri Lanka), good "runs shore", and an interesting visit to Hiroshima. One of my favourite parts of the diary is the story of my father being a drinks waiter at one of the ship's cocktail parties where he got rather drunk (how he managed to serve drinks in that state and not receive 'punishment' I've no idea!) - oh how I wish I could have been at that cocktail party, I bet it was a blast.

Another insight was to see how my father's 'love language' of the giving of gifts was strong in him even as a young 22-23 year old. My father was not particularly demonstrative in an affectionate way or good at expressing his love and affection with words, but he always expressed his love by giving presents or money to my mother, his children and grandchildren. During his trip, he bought my mother underwear, a blouse, a set of pearls, a Kimono and a music box - all his way of showing her love (even though he records he forgot to send her a birthday card) - these gifts were the expression of his deep love for her. Maybe it was presenting her with all these gifts that changed her mind about marrying him.

My father died in August 2010, aged 79. My mother died in January 2018 aged 82.

The diary has now passed down to my father's eldest grandson - Ben - and rightly so. And there's no more fitting conclusion to this diary than Ben's Eulogy to his grandfather, which sums up so poignantly the effects of trauma and pain:

> This, this is all new and oh so strange
> The world you once knew has drastically changed
> You look confused yet you know so much
> Your mind's still here but you're out of touch.
>
> Don't worry my lifelong family and friend
> You'll be happier in the end
> Going back to what you know
> The days when winters still had snow.
>
> I've seen your pain, I know your hurt
> But not many men can stake your claim

Take your memories or steal your fame
And you were young in love and strong at heart
And this is your chance to go back to the start.

These waves will carry you homeward bound
He's heard your distress call lost but now found
I'm going to live my life to the full
Just as you did out on the hull
And I know someday we'll be together again
And I love you so much, your grandson, Ben.

God bless.

# ACKNOWLEDGEMENT

I would like to thank Ray Thomas for his permission to use photographs and material from his wonderful website (and also for sharing my father's diary on there). Here is the link to Ray's website for anyone wishing to explore the interesting historical information he has recorded: **www.brisray.com/dad/**

I would like to thank my nephew Ben Palethorpe for the loan of my father's diary enabling me to type it up, and also thank my sister Elizabeth Palethorpe for sending me many photos.

My thanks to Michel Nelis for use of his image taken at Yokohama War Cemetary.

Any omissions will be corrected in future editions - otherwise, as far as I know, all other material is in the public domain.

Printed in Great Britain
by Amazon